Libya's Destiny

Sways between

<u>Arab Spring</u>
<u>And</u>
<u>Pendulum Swings</u>

By **GO PAL**

THIS BOOK IS SEQUEL TO MY PUBLICATION

"GADDAFI UP –CLOSE"

Prologue

This book covers the historical past of Libya, including the early 1900s when the world acclaimed hero ,
OMAR MUKHTAR -"THE LION OF THE DESERT"
fought against the Mussolini gang's war machinery, on a horseback.

They were outnumbered, unequipped, untrained and gave all they got.

They gave the Italian army a taste of their superior agility, guerilla techniques, and gutsy wherewithal. They orchestrated determined pitched battles, against the ruthless marauders, who were cowardly. The Italian armed battalions tortured the unarmed kids and women, using huge well-equipped tanks, canons, and were hell bent upon burning their rations and huts. The army General forced the poor civilian nomads into fenced concentration camps.

They raped and tortured the hopelessly helpless forcing them to disclose Omar's whereabouts and openly used these tactics to weaken Omar's will to fight until death, but failed miserably for over 20 years. Finally when he was captured, he was dragged behind a jeep, with hands and feet shackled in heavy steel chains, for several miles in the hot desert and brought to the stunningly beautiful Mediterranean seashores.

He was asked to surrender, was tempted with a huge salary, high rank, and gold coins. He refused all the time, every time. As a final technique of torture he was tempted with drinking water and when he put forward his hands, he was kicked and the officers drank the water and threw the rest in the sand. He was finally hanged in front of his followers.

Gaddafi fills this book with chapters describing his 42 years as an extremely powerful ruler.

Gaddafi's ruling life in Libya was full of huge UP-&-DOWN swings.

He was born a revolutionary and died as one. In 1969 he was the torch holder, but in 2011 he was tortured. He was on the receiving end of the brutalities (including sodomy) which to my mind reflects the type of depraved people who will effect Libya's Future Destiny.

The first eight months of his rapid rise to power were unique and remarkably outstanding, in the long political history of Libya.

He dethroned King Idris during the week the later was under treatment in a European hospital. Idris had no offspring from his marriage. Basically he was a weak ruler –a mere puppet in the hands of western powers, especially Great Britain, and a pleasure-loving debauch of the Sennusi Clan-the very clan to which Omar Mukhtar had brought the highest respect and honor!

Gaddafi neither fired a single bullet nor allowed any legal repercussions to ensue! He quickly teamed up with 10 young Army Officers and mounted a peaceful Coup-d'état. He also nullified Idris' Royal Order ensuring his throne to his nephew. This drove a death knell to any legal wrangling.

He quickly established himself as Libya's commander in chief as well as chairman of the Revolutionary Command Council. He cleverly blended Arab nationalism, revolutionary socialism, and Islamic orthodoxy, all three of which covered the prevalent mindset of the total Libyan population. This helped him lead the country as their undisputed popular leader from 1969 onwards.

The last 8 months of his waning power ended in his brutal assassination.

Only he was brave enough to withstand such a shameful end. He stood his grounds, refused to hide or run away till the last day! These 8 months are described in the chapters that follow. There are several other chapters on the Geography and History of the country and comparing its Government with other nations which reflect on its past.

The future of Libya has been visualized through a variety of possible international interference. Interesting and illuminating chapters link its oil, as a bounty desired by several western nations.

Diversity of its tribal disunity, the rebel nomads, Libya's Geography, list of Tourists attractions, and other diverse subjects played a part in Libya's tryst with destiny.

The last chapter on Green-less Golf Course in Sand and storm is a must read.

EVEN GOD FORGOT ABOUT LIBYA!

As it has become self apparent that there is no solitary positive and invincible prediction for Libya's future in this very small exercise, which I have spent days on end to solve. However in the universe of the Big Bangs, the Black Holes and self-destroying Heat Death, this is an infinitesimally minute nano-metric nanosecond problem. While the almighty God had on his hands, the massive Cosmos scenarios like doubling the universe several times in a split second, he forgot about the little Libya.

Some mysteries of the universe were partially discovered in the huge Hubble observatories and other theorized by the brilliant mathematicians, like Albert Einstein. However several famous scientists, cosmologists, physicists, astronauts, cosmonauts subsequently proved them wrong by later researches. Some well known amongst them were Newton, Kelvin, Edwin Hubble, Stephen Hawkins, Alan Guth, Dr Michio Kaku, James Gunn, Christopher Doppler, Prof. Krauss, Wilkinson, and Moshe Carmeli to name a few!

The intermediary beliefs that BIG BANG took place 15 billion years ago; STARS existed 10 billion years ago; SUN 5 billion years back; MOLTEN EARTH 4.5 billion years ago, depended on the time in history when these were propagated!

Moons/Stars tell us the story of our existence. Our galaxy has eight planets. There are 300 moons in the universe and around the solar system. Jupiter and Saturn have 60 moons each.

The BIBLE says the STARS were created in 3 days, and UNIVERSE was created in 6 days.

Some Christians claim it as evidence for God using the Big Bang to create, but this causes a huge controversy, since Genesis has the earth before the Sun, whereas the Big bang has the sun millions of years before the earth. It is no wonder the Big Bang-Christian scientists proved the six- days earth-rotation theory to be wrong!

The Big Bang involves the earth cooling down for millions of years, rather than being covered with water at the beginning as Genesis teaches. They also therefore promote millions of years of Earth history, placing death, and disease well prior to the fall of Adam.

Dark Energy

'The accelerating power of the universe is not the result of Dark Energy, but God's Almighty power as He gave impetus to the universe'- John Hartnett.

The enormity of the factors beyond our control; the lack of knowledge about what tomorrow shall bring; the unpredictability about the future of our own galaxy and how long it shall last, increases our faith in a higher authority and brings people with artificial ego down a peg or two.

Having diverted attention from the challenge at hand viz. Libya's Destiny I ventured into the study of our own little "EARTH."

The land is only a small part of the conglomeration of oceans and seven seas. The rapid pace of scientific developments, and the speed of travel, has beaten the speed of sound and not that of light yet. So much so that we have started calling the mighty Atlantic Ocean –"a pond?"

All wars, including WW1, WW2 etc. end in poverty, discord, long lasting hatred, and economic disaster. Killing innocent civilians, children, helpless females and unarmed bystanders on both sides. I do not understand why humanity pays a huge price for these conflicts,?

The madness, ego, and greed led the Japanese warlords to bombard American warships in Midway and Pearl Harbor, without any provocation. The end result was the dropping of Atom Bombs on Hiroshima, resulting from the burning spirit of revenge and hatred. This caused the death of innocent millions and destruction of their property and belongings as an unintended consequence.

What did they do to earn and receive such dire punishment and ending?

Certainly it was the violent act of a few that caused, misery and death to millions who were peacefully and innocently minding their own business and were never supportive of the policies of the evil dictators and marauders to start with!

The hopeless and helpless millions of innocent people including children were mercilessly killed in minutes.

I strongly believe there is an aura of glory and worship surrounding the victors from the days of the caveman, the victors were worshipped, be it the terrorist like Genghis Khan, the warriors like the Romans, Alexander the Great, Herr Mussolini, Madman Herr Hitler, and hundreds others. Even in democratic America the war presidents get several terms to reign! Power rises to crush Power to gain Power and the vicious cycle behaves like an unstoppable revolving door. The whole cycle is a continuous curse.

The ego and glory blinds man till he deteriorates to the level of an animal. Animals cannot have any element of dignity or respect for others. They have never been taught to live and let live. They are only interested to fulfil their hunger, pounce mercilessly on their prey, using all thinkable tricks from the nature's book e.g. the prowess, the speed, the camouflage, experience, instinct and several God given abilities used by the underwater predators in the vast ocean we know so little about! A pair of tigers killed a female rhino while she was having difficulty birthing a calf. The Kaziranga Park staff removed her horn after she died to prevent poachers from pouncing on them. You notice that neither the tigers nor the poachers would ever bother about the birthing difficulty of the childbearing rhino. There is a Jungle out there and it seems to be engulfing the world. It would take brilliant statesmanship and an almighty effort to reverse this trend. Only wisdom shall prevail.

Of course there is always a contrary school of thought propagating two theories a) The survival of the fittest and b) Natures balancing act of controlling the run-away population by the rule of the jungle.

What is really the distinction between the Animal kingdom and us where the survival of the fittest and Nature's might keeps in check any excessive population? While I was pouring my thoughts on this page I couldn't help listening to the BRIEFING of AL JAZEERA BBC NEWS.

Suicide bombers (hoping to get a dozen virgins in heaven) killed 18 people on their way to break the *Ramadan Fast* near the gates of the Algeria's Military Academy.

African Union refused to recognize the National Transitional Council as a legitimate body to rule Libya, without a treaty with the present head of the state, Col. Gaddafi.

Mexico's Drug Lords are mercilessly killing locals and tourists to keep the Drug smuggling routes open and clear. Five hundred and fifty people had disappeared on the border in just a day. The dead bodies were so mutilated that they could not be recognized.

The Anti Graft watchdog Anna Hazare in India is keeping Fast-Unto-Death, until the parliament passes strict Anti-Corruption rules. There has not been any resolution to this unfortunate stalemate. The truth is that the corruption is so widespread and out of control.

At least 18 people were killed and dozens injured some critically, in a car bombing at the UN Headquarters in the Nigerian capital Abuja.

NATO air strikes have been targeting Col. Gaddafi's forces, acting on a UN mandate to protect civilians. But I feel the unintended consequences could result in killing several innocent stand-byes or human shields instead.

The oncoming Hurricane Irene in Northeast Coast of USA and Floods in Mandool Phillipines are causing damages costing millions of dollars.

Japanese Prime Minister resigns today, due to economic woes.

There is never good news, because newscasters thrive on sensationalism.

The chapter on the Haves and Have-Nots has shown us the start of awakening of the younger generation of boys and girls, majority of whom had no jobs, gathered in a non-violent assembly in the Central City Square in Cairo. Their target was the billionaire President Hosni Mubarak who accumulated wealth like a King. After 18 days of suppressing peaceful protesters, the soldiers fraternized with them and slowly but surely the massive street protests gathered momentum and the President was forced out. But democratic chaos ensued.

This success caught the imagination of almost all other Middle Eastern countries with huge income disparities between the rich and poor, during the "ARAB SPRING." When awakening filtered through to the Libyan masses, they started and fizzled out near Benghazi, because as I told my friends that Libya is different. I have lived there and seen how Gaddafi operates. From times immemorial, an individual has always found comfort in, and desired to have company. Amongst humans the biggest punishment for a wrongdoer and a prisoner of war has been " To lock him up in a compact hole without the ability to use one's senses of Seeing, Talking, Smelling, Listening or Doing things with others. The animals in a jungle, the fish in the sea, the birds in the air, and us humans all have something in common:

The Almighty Brain to Think.
The Heart to Love and fill with Desire.
The Nose to Smell a Rose.
The Ears to listen to the Symphony.
The Legs to run to meet a friend.
The Arms to hug which would kill any Grudge.
I can fill up hundreds of pages of books and still not be able to completely express the-
Infinite mysteries of nature, that the
"God Almighty" (or the supernatural power you may believe in,) has created in the whole universe:

The Dwellers in the seas, skies, and the oceans have a common purpose:

To unite and to co-exist in harmony and those who leave the team or misbehave shall die in isolation.

The kingdom below the ocean is so vast that thousands of research scholars and individuals have studied about its mysterious creatures and their characteristics for past hundreds of years and only scratched the surface. Quoting a few discoveries here, that the ocean floor is full of aquatic nonvascular plants, seaweed, stone- worts, algae rich in chlorophyll often masked by brown or red pigments. The mighty white Shark has been gifted with the natural power to smell out blood 200 feet away. These marine elasmobranch fishes have a fusiform body, lateral bronchial clefts, and a tough skin roughened by minute tubercles. Their large livers are a source of oil and their hide is a source of leather. The typical predators are sometimes dangerous to humans.

Submicroscopic agents consist of extremely complex molecules that typically contain a protein coat surrounding an RNA or DNA of genetic material that are capable of multiplying only in living cells, causing various important discoveries in man, under water animals (like Sharks, Rays, Chimaeras,) bacterial virus and plants.

On the other extreme the world population, growing faster than the available resources for survival, created famines. This however eliminated the wrong people. The almighty nature then created the self-evolving and self-resolving principle of the survival of the fittest, using the weaker as the food to satisfy the hunger of the stronger and faster. The laws of the jungle and the vast oceans had been established and maintained using the tools suitable for the tasks. Over time the Lion had taken over as the king of the Jungle, the mighty pythons and cobras ruled the underground creatures, the mighty Eagles flew above others in the air and the almighty white sharks were vastly feared in the oceans.

The almighty knows and remembers all the variety of trillions of living things and more. But do not forget that plants, trees and every thing imaginable has life as well. This is proven beyond doubt by the enormous variety of colors and the way they develop into joyful shapes as they grow day and night helped by the air, sun, the rain and even in the dark. Do not forget the Grizzly Bear, the Snowbird, the Penguins, and the Polar Bear who needs *SNOW to GROW*.

I am sure you got my point, that amongst humans too there was Adam and Eve that gave us life, in spite of the forbidden apple. Then came the institution of Marriage. Simultaneously elements of society on the opposite side, like,

The *GAYS, LESBIANS, AMBISEXTROUS, CHILD MOLESTERS, PORNOGRAPHERS, PEDOPHILES, AND RAPISTS* existed in ever increasing numbers amongst all groups of human assemblies (and believe it or not secretly amongst some Padres, Brahmins, Mullahs, and the traders in human flesh.)

In recent years there has been, increasing number of divorces. Now and again there are groupings *FOR and AGAINST* Same-Sex Marriages.

Coming straight on to the system of

MAN CONTROLLING OTHER HUMANS

There has been several systems evolving over the ages. Starting with our aboriginal four legged chimps, and for that matter the whole of the animal kingdom staying in herds to show solidarity and strength, to fight the fear and to keep vigil (taking turns,) against threats from the predators.

Our so-called forefathers passed on to us the very instincts, of self-preservation, survival, and above all the Herd instinct. There were the Cave men, the Gladiators, the Cannibals, Followed by the Hunters, the Marauders, and the imaginary Draculas, amongst our aborigines, through the ages.

The human weaknesses took charge of our history and various complexes overtook us.

The complex of *FEAR*, of *GREED*, of *ANGER*, of *TRUST*, *CAMARADERIE*, and *SUPERSTITION* controlled our brains. There were a few amongst us who had superior skills and brains from birth. Some of us still believe it to be a gift from *GOD*. That created a few natural leaders amongst us, yielding a huge populace of followers.

With the advent of time the *GLOBE* became compartmentalized into various geographical subdivisions. The *WEST*, the *EAST*, and the *MIDDLE EAST* have turned out to be the major landmasses in recent history. There is also the *SOUTHERN OCEAN-O-SPHERE* with several important islands, countries. *THE SNOW CAPPED MIGHTY MOUNTAINS, CANADA, RUSSIA,* and several countries that separated from USSR. Then there are,

THE NORTH AND SOUTH POLES.

History produced several hegemonic tyrants who were so egotistic, self-centered, and empowered by greed that they wanted to enslave the whole world.

The Genghis Khans, the Hitler, Alexander the Great of the world, who used power and wars to destroy their opposition and gain more power. However another superior Power killed theirs' and restarted that particular vicious cycle all over again. But the present world we live in consists of 207 countries under different systems of governance.

Some information, has been taken from various articles

Within Wikipedia, but this information can change with the fluidity of the political climate, around the world.

Since the fall of the Roman Empire, several other Power blocks formed out of hegemony have come and gone. There were empires built on the supremacy of Sea Power, in the old days. British used to rule India (including Pakistan) for 360 years, and their empire had spread all over the world. It was often said that the sun never sets on the British Empire and now it hardly rises even in U.K.

Since then failed attempts of hegemony by Japan, Russia through Communism, Hitler through Fascism, and several religious harmony, like the Roman Catholics, built separate Vatican state, but nothing lasts for ever. Democracy seems to be winning, for the time being. It too cannot last forever. The effected countries resented the system of American interference. Their population joined under religious flags and the winds of poverty, and the forces of hatred and animosity sparked off another war. These wars unfortunately kill the poor and innocent at a young age and leave behind non-coherent groups who continue their discontent for another century or two. Thus the peace is short-lived, and the pendulum re-swings. Even while I am writing these pages the governments in Egypt and Tunisia have changed, and Gaddafi is on his way out.

The various types of systems of governance, can also change in the future, because I feel the hegemony by USA and allied countries is supported by a) Superior Air Power, b) Superior technological development and c) Economic Strength.

Change in any of these, especially due to the shaking up of the fiscal and monetary policy, or over leveraging in housing loans and falling stock markets can lead to disunity and disharmony in the world trade. This in turn can result in already depressed economy, burst through its seams! The existence of Euro is already being threatened!

Gaddafi had a "never to be left behind" gumption and just to outdo the West, had put up the most advanced and very large capacity TELESCOPE, worth several hundred millions. God also kept his mind diverted to petty battles and he was petty minded in not allowing his people to be educated.

Hence the title of this chapter that even God forgot about Little Libya?

THE NOMADS:
LIBYA'S HERITAGE &
HISTORY

From centuries past, Libyan tribes have PRESERVED their historical lineage.

The inter-relations and/or rift between each other was suppressed during the Gaddafi regime but has resurfaced and is getting worst.

The geographic and transportation hurdles to reunite them are only part of the problem. The lack of education, the religious diversity, and poverty are factors that will play a role in the future progress, or lack there of in the country as a whole.

Gaddafi's propaganda machine and his techniques, of buying people's goodwill by donating free living quarters, goods, and money are gone with him.

Tuaregs are a nomadic Berber tribe from central Sahara. They live in Algeria, Mali, Niger, Libya, and Burkina Faso. Tuareg rebellions broke out in 1990 and 2000 after the Nigerian and Malian governments attempted to absorb the tribes into their jurisdiction. This prompted a mass Tuareg exodus towards Algeria and Libya.

Assan Midal

"With the crisis currently sweeping the country, life has become very expensive in Libya. Most Tuareg sedentary families in the

Sebha desert region can no longer make ends meet. The economy is paralyzed. Those who had low-paid work, such as cleaning or street vending, all lost their jobs. They can no longer earn a living, so most are returning home before the situation worsens."

Most of the people who came back from Libya refuse to share their views on the current conflict, even though they seem very well informed on recent developments. They don't want to take sides. What worries them is that they may no longer have jobs. Although the mass demonstrations in Syria have shaken one of the most authoritarian regimes in the Middle East, the opposition has made no major gains in recent months. It holds no territory and has no clear leadership.

Tuareg rebellion leaders are committed to Gaddafi's cause after the rebellions of 1990 and 2000, the Libyan leader acted as a mediator between tribes and local governments.

Libyan nomads gave up Gaddafi's son despite €1m offer.

It is unclear if Hotmani had planned to ensnare Saif al-Islam from the moment he linked up with the fugitive's group in the Sahara desert, or if he defected when he had doubts about his payment and feared he might be killed.

The Saharan nomad, who calls himself the "son of the desert" refused to give details on when or how he contacted the 15 fighters of the interim government who caught Saif al-Islam.

There was less than $5,000 found in the two-car convoy and Hotmani said he was not paid a penny of the €1 million promised to him.

LIBYA'S HISTORY

Libya is an African country in the Maghreb region of North Africa bordered by the Mediterranean Sea to the north, Egypt to the east, Sudan to the southeast, Chad and Niger to the south, and Algeria and Tunisia to the west.

With an area of almost 1.8 million square kilometers (700,000 sq. mi.), Libya is the fourth largest country in Africa by area, and the 17th largest in the world. The largest city, Tripoli, is home to 1.7 million of Libya's 6.4 million people. The three traditional parts of the country are Tripolitania, Fezzan and Cyrenaica.

In 2009 Libya had the fourth highest GDP per capita in Africa, behind Seychelles, Equatorial Guinea and Gabon. Libya has the 10th-largest proven oil reserves of any country in the world and the 17th-highest petroleum production.
Sahara desert, which now covers roughly 90% of Libya, was lush with green vegetation tens of thousands of years ago. It was home to lakes, forests, diverse wildlife, and a temperate Mediterranean climate, during 500 BC to 500 AD.
5900 years later with the onset of intense aridness the Green Sahara rapidly transformed into the Sahara Desert as you see today.

Archaeological evidence indicates that Neolithic peoples from as early as 8000 BC, inhabited the coastal plain of Ancient Libya. These peoples were perhaps drawn by the climate, which enabled their culture to grow.

The Ancient Libyans were skilled in the domestication of cattle and the cultivation of crops.

17

Rock paintings and carvings at Wadi Mathendous and the mountainous region of Jebel Acacus are the best sources of information about prehistoric Libya, and the pastoral culture that settled there. The paintings reveal that the Libyan Sahara contained rivers, grassy plateaus, and an abundance of wildlife such as giraffes, elephants, and crocodiles.

Pockets of the Berber populations have spread in most of modern Libya. Desertification, caused by changes in the climate, resulted in massive dispersal of the Nomad population, from the Atlantic coast in Libya to the Siwa Oasis in Egypt. It is thought that the indigenous Libyan civilization of the Garamantes, based in Germa, originated around the period, while the Sahara was still green.

The Garamantes were a Saharan people of Berber origin who used an elaborate underground irrigation system, and founded a kingdom in the Fezzan area of modern-day Libya. They were probably present as tribal people in the Fezzan by 1000 BC, and were a local power in the Sahara between 500 BC and 500 AD. By the time of contact with the Phoenicians, the first of the Semitic civilizations to arrive in Libya from the East, the Lebu, Garamantes, Bebers and other tribes that lived in the Sahara were already well established.
The Phoenicians were the first to establish trading posts in Libya, when the merchants of Tyre (in present-day Lebanon) developed commercial relations with the Berber tribes and made treaties with them to ensure their cooperation in the exploitation of raw materials.
By the fifth century BC, the greatest of the Phoenician colonies, Carthage, had extended its hegemony across much of North Africa, where a distinctive civilization, known as Punic, came into being. Punic settlements on the Libyan coast included Oea (later Tripoli), Libdah (later Leptis Magna), and Sabratha. These cities were in an area that was later called Tripolis, or "Three

Cities" from which Libya's modern capital Tripoli takes its name.

In 630 BC, the Ancient Greeks colonized Eastern Libya and founded the city of Cyrene. Within 200 years, four more important Greek cities were established in the area that became known as Cyrenaica: Barce (later Marj); Euhesperides (later Berenice, present-day Benghazi); Taucheira (later Arsinoe, present-day Taucheria); Balagrae (later Bayda and Beda Littoria under Italian occupation, present-day Bayda); and Apollonia (later Susa), the port of Cyrene.
Together with Cyrene, they were known as the Pentapolis (Five Cities). Cyrene became one of the greatest intellectual and artistic centers of the Greek world, and was famous for its medical school, learned academies, and architecture.
The Greeks of the Pentapolis resisted encroachments by the Ancient Egyptians from the East, as well as by the Carthaginians from the West, but in 525 BC the Persian army of Cambyses II overran Cyrenaica, which for the next two centuries remained under Persian or Egyptian rule. Alexander the Great was greeted by the Greeks when he entered Cyrenaica in 331 BC, and Eastern Libya again fell under the control of the Greeks, this time as part of the Ptolemaic Kingdom.
Later, a federation of the Pentapolis was formed that was customarily ruled by a king drawn from the Ptolemaic royal house.
After the fall of Carthage the Romans did not occupy Tripolitania (the region around Tripoli) immediately, but left it under control of the kings of Numidia, until the coastal cities asked and obtained its protection. Ptolemy Apion, the last Greek ruler, bequeathed Cyrenaica to Rome, which formally annexed the region in 74 BC and joined it to Crete as a Roman province.

The decline of the Roman Empire saw the classical cities fall into ruin, a process hastened by the Vandals' destructive sweep though North Africa in the 5th century.

The region's prosperity had shrunk under Vandal domination, and the old Roman political and social order, disrupted by the Vandals, could not be restored.

In outlying areas neglected by the Vandals, the inhabitants had sought the protection of tribal chieftains and, having grown accustomed to their autonomy, resisted re-assimilation into the imperial system.

Tenuous Byzantine control over Libya was restricted to a few poorly defended coastal strongholds.

The Arab horsemen who first crossed into the Pentapolis of Cyrenaica in September 642 AD, encountered little resistance under the command of 'Amr ibn al-'as, the armies of Islam conquered Cyrenaica, and renamed the Pentapolis, Barqa.

They also marched into Tripoli, but after destroying the Roman walls of the city and getting a tribute they withdrew.

In 647 an army of 40,000 Arabs, led by Abdullah Ibn Saad, the foster-brother of Caliph Uthman, penetrated deep into Western Libya and took Tripoli from the Byzantines. The Fezzan (Libya's Southern region) was conquered by Uqba ibn Nafi in 663 after crushing the Berber resistance.

In the centuries that followed Libya came under the rule of several Islamic dynasties, under various levels of autonomy. The largest Caliphates of the time were Ummayad, Abbasid and Fatimid. Arab rule was easily imposed in the coastal farming areas and on the towns, which again prospered under the Arab patronage. Townsmen valued the security that permitted them to practice their commerce and trade in peace, while the Punicized farmers recognized their affinity with the Semitic Arabs to whom they looked to protect their lands. In Cyrenaica, Monophysite adherents of the Coptic Church had welcomed the Muslim Arabs as liberators from Byzantine oppression. The Berber tribes of the hinterland accepted Islam, however they resisted Arab political rule.

For the next several decades, Libya was under the purview of the Ummayad Caliph of Damascus until the Abbasids overthrew the Ummayads in 750, and Libya came under the rule of Baghdad. (A far cry from Saddam vs. Gaddafi of modern times and both mercilessly assassinated!)
When Caliph Harun al-Rashid appointed Ibrahim ibn al-Aghlab as his governor of Ifriqiya in 800, Libya enjoyed considerable local autonomy under the Aghlabid dynasty. The Aghlabids were amongst the most attentive Islamic rulers of Libya.
They brought about a measure of order to the region, and restored Roman irrigation systems, which brought prosperity to the area from the agricultural surplus.
After a successful invasion by the Habsburgs of Spain in the early 16th century, Charles V entrusted its defense to the Knights of St. John in Malta.
Lured by the piracy that spread through the Maghreb coastline, adventurers such as Barbarossa and his successors consolidated Ottoman control in the central Maghreb.
The Ottoman Turks conquered Tripoli in 1551 under the command of Sinan Pasha.

Tripoli was the only city of size in Ottoman Libya (then known as Tripolitania Eyalet) at the end of the 17th century and had a population of about 30,000.

The bulk of its residents were Moors- popularly known as the city-dwelling Arabs.

Several hundred Turks and renegades formed a governing elite, a large portion of which was kouloughlis (lit. sons of servants— offspring of Turkish soldiers and Arab women.)

They identified with local interests and were respected by locals.

Jews and Moriscos were active as merchants and craftsmen and a small number of European traders also frequented the city. European slaves and large numbers of enslaved blacks transported from Sudan was also a feature of everyday life in Tripoli.

In 1551, Turgut Reis enslaved almost the entire population of the Maltese Island of Gozo.

The most pronounced slavery activity involved the enslavement of black Africans who were brought via Trans-Saharan trade routes. Even though the slave trade was officially abolished in Tripoli in 1853, in practice it continued until the 1890s.

War broke out between the United States and Tripolitania, in the early 19th century and a series of battles ensued in what came to be known as the Barbary Wars.
By 1819, the various treaties of the Napoleonic Wars had forced the Barbary States to give up piracy almost entirely, and Tripolitania's economy began to crumble.

European colonial interests set their eyes on the marginal Turkish provinces of Libya.

Reunification came about through the unlikely route of an invasion (Italo-Turkish War, 1911–1912) and occupation starting from 1911 when Italy simultaneously turned the three regions into colonies.

From 1927 to 1934, the territory was split into two colonies, Italian Cyrenaica and Italian Tripolitania, run by Italian governors. Some 150,000 Italians settled in Libya, constituting roughly 20% of the total population.

In 1934, Italy adopted the name "Libya" (used by the Greeks for all of North Africa, except Egypt) as the official name of the colony (made up of the three provinces of Cyrenaica, Tripolitania and Fezzan).

Idris al-Mahdi as-Senussi (later King Idris I), Emir of Cyrenaica, led Libyan resistance to Italian occupation between the two world wars.
Ilan Pappé estimates that between 1928 and 1932 the Italian military "killed half the Bedouin population (directly or through disease and starvation in camps)."
Italian historian Emilio Gentile estimated the number of victims of the repression to 50,000.
From 1943 to 1951, Tripolitania and Cyrenaica were under British administration, while the French controlled Fezzan. In 1944, Idris returned from exile in Cairo but declined to resume permanent residence in Cyrenaica until the removal of some aspects of foreign control in 1947. Under the terms of the 1947 peace treaty with the Allies, Italy relinquished all claims to Libya.

Libya declared its independence as the United Kingdom of Libya, a constitutional and hereditary monarchy under King Idris, Libya's first and only monarch.

Libyan Constitution was enacted in 1951. It did not create a secular state but it formally set out the following rights under Article 5:

Islam was proclaimed as the religion of the State. Every one is the same in the eyes of Law and justice.

Equal civil and political rights. Equal opportunities, and an equal responsibility for public duties and obligations. "Without distinction of religion, belief, race, language, wealth, kinship or political or social opinions."

The discovery of significant oil reserves in 1959 and the subsequent income from petroleum sales enabled one of the world's poorest nations to establish an extremely wealthy state. Although oil drastically improved the Libyan government's finances, resentment among some factions began to build over the increased concentration of the nation's wealth in the hands of King Idris. This discontent mounted with the rise of Nasserism and Arab nationalism throughout North Africa and the Middle East, so while the continued presence of Americans, Italians and British in Libya aided in the increased levels of wealth and tourism following WWII, it was seen by some as a threat.

During this period, Britain was involved in extensive engineering projects in Libya and was also the country's biggest supplier of arms. The United States also maintained the large Wheelus Air Base in Libya.

PENDULUM
SWINGS

Libya's Destiny in post-Gaddafi era can best be predicted, by studying its past. That is exactly what this book does.

The Obama administration acted in a politically correct manner by keeping a NATO cushion between themselves and the ground warfare between Gaddafi supporters and the rebels. They stayed away from direct confrontation in the air, using NATO countries as buffer, and no western power openly aided and abetted in the ground conflicts between opposing Libyan faction. This swing of the pendulum was 180° apart from Bush's handling of the Iraq affair.

Obama was actually voted into power due to the anti-Bush sentiment prevailing at that juncture.

However the way Assama Bin Laden, was fed into the ocean's predators, was caused by the timely use of modern scientific knowledge, of remote positioning of the target by drones and perfect details developed by the GOOGLE mapping-another brilliant scientific achievement aided by the satellite. The pendulum has swung afresh and Gaddafi's assassination was

possible using same techniques. The credit goes to Leon Panetta, brought in by Obama
to replace Robert Gates!

I think Obama is like that cool cat, or better still the smart cool monkey who makes hay, while the two cats fight. I am referring to the childhood story my Granny Nanny used to tell me at bedtime where the two cats were fighting over unfair division of the cake they wanted to share equally. The monkey convinced them that he would cut the cake equally. He swindled them by cutting one half-bigger and eating the smaller piece. He repeated same process and continued eating the scrapped smaller pieces till he gobbled the whole cake. Now they had nothing to fight for.

Republicans are the only party that could remove him from the White House, but because they have introduced another joker in the pack called the *TEA PARTY*, the potential candidates are fighting for the nomination like the proverbial cats-and Obama is sitting pretty. He was virtually voted into power by *President Bush* (a republican) and may stay in power because of the continued disunity in the opposition party cats?

While *BUSH, McCAINE, DICK CHENEY* and dozens of Republicans who like the then *Defense Secretary DONALD RUMSFELD*, the architect of the torture chambers at Guantanamo Bay in the Castro Country, were swinging the Pendulum on the opposing side, building tons of hatred against America. They wasted the lives of thousands of American soldiers, and banned the media from photographing the dead bodies of American heroes and publishing the news about, the beloved countrymen who sacrificed their lives for the defense of their country. At the same time The Queen personally honored British heroes dead bodies with multiple guns salute, and more. Bush wars also burnt to ashes, trillions of dollars of the money USA had borrowed. They brought the economy to an almost a recessional halt, and raised taxes for the middle and lower classes, while reducing those for the top 1%.

26

Obama on the other hand used the drones and special well-knit Swat teams to slowly assassinate and secretly bury the Gaddafi and the Osamas of the world. Yesterday he quietly got rid of another most wanted Al Qaida leader by a drone attack. His technique is so cool that he disintegrates, or secretly buries the dead despots to eliminate any contact with their devotees. Hence he avoided whipping up further hatred against USA, so far.

His recent foreign policy (see the news below), of countervailing India against Pakistan and China leaves more questions than clarity? So far it is not easy to decipher?

Admiral Robert Willard wants India to Serve as USA's "ECONOMIC ANCHOR" in Asia.

Sustaining US Global Leadership (a priority for 21st Century Defense) identifies China as a security threat to the US in long term!

I have heard several times from some Chinese Industrial leaders that they are feeding USA-I believe they loan us several billions of dollars!

The US forces will no longer be sized to conduct open wars at two separate fronts simultaneously.

As long as nuclear weapons exist the USA will maintain a safe, secure and effective arsenal. They will try to enforce other allied nations to do the same. They will ensure that Axis of evil do not obtain the resources and/or build up capabilities of such an arsenal under their control!

In the aftermath of the Iraq and Afghan wars USA will emphasize and endeavor to use non-military means and military-to-military cooperation to address instability issues. They will continue to lead global efforts in strengthening international norms of responsible behavior and maintain interoperable military capabilities.

Panetta counts India as a Challenge. China and India are the two rising powers in Asia. While USA has powerful presence in the Pacific, China is a rising force to reckon with! The Secretary strongly values a close military relationship with India-a nation of increasing prominence and power.

USA wants to be able to have a flexible, adaptable, agile force that can deal with a myriad of challenges in today's world.

Obama identifies China as one of the major security threats to America in the long run, and puts Asia on a higher priority. Thus a long-term strategic alliance between USA and INDIA is becoming a near possibility and a priority.

INDIA HANDS OVER $1 MILLION IN CASH TO LIBYAN National Transitional Council. This was transmitted through the United Nation's Office of Commissioner for Humanitarian Aid in New York.
India is also sending:
$1 million worth in life saving medicines and medical equipment.
and dispatching a team of "Jaipur Foot," to Tripoli to provide prostheses (artificial limbs,) to the injured Libyans, at a center being set up there.

Violence is not merely killing another.

It is violence when we use a sharp word,

When we make a gesture to brush away a person,

When we obey because there is   fear.

So violence isn't merely organized butchery

In the name of God,

In the name of society, or country.

Violence is much more subtle, much deeper,

and we are inquiring into

the very depths of violence.

Krishnamurti.

♀ ♀ ♀

LEADERSHIP AND CONTROL

Libya's Destiny will to a large extent depend upon the speed with which well-established law & order returns, and a powerful, popular system of governance completely free from foreign influence is established here.

Libyan people are well advised to
Pursue peace and Stay away from the evils of revenge, and hatred.

In our little world there is no prevailing peace and harmony and there exist several methods and systems of governance as listed below:
Systems of Government
And the countries following them:

A Republic, with Executive Head of State
And Presidency being independent of Legislature.

Afghanistan, Angola, Argentina, Armenia, Azerbaijan, Belarus, Benin, Bolivia, Brazil, Burundi, Cameron, Central African Republic, Chad, Chile, Colombia, Comoros, Costa Rica, Cyprus, Dominican Republic, Ecuador, El Salvador, Equatorial Guinea, Gabon, The Gambia, Ghana, Guatemala, Guinea, Honduras, Indonesia, Iran, Kazakhstan, Kiribati, Liberia, Malawi, Maldives, Mexico, Mozambique, Myanmar, Namibia, Nicaragua, Nigeria, Palau, Panama, Paraguay, Peru, Philippines, Republic of the Congo, Rwanda, Seychelles, Sierra Leone, South Korea, South Sudan, Sudan, Suriname, Switzerland, Tanzania, Togo, Tunisia,
Uganda, Ukraine, United States, Uruguay, Uzbekistan, Venezuela, Yemen, Zambia.

A Republic, with Ceremonial Head of State and Ministry being subjected To parliamentary confidence.

Albania, Austria, Bangladesh, Bosnia and Herzegovina, Bulgaria, Cape Verde, Croatia, Czech republic, Dominica, East Timor, Estonia, Ethiopia, Finland, Germany, Greece, Hungary, Iceland, India, Iraq, Ireland, Israel, Italy, Latvia, Lebanon, Macedonia, Malta, Mauritius, Moldova, Montenegro, Nepal, Pakistan, Poland, Samoa, San Marino, Serbia, Singapore, Slovakia, Slovenia, Trinidad and Tobago, Turkey, Vanuatu.,

A Constitutional Monarchy, with

Ceremonial Head of State, And Ministry being subjected to parliamentary confidence.

Andorra, Antigua and Barbuda, Australia, The Bahamas, Barbados, Belgium, Belize, Cambodia, Canada, Denmark, Grenada, Jamaica, Japan, Lesotho, Luxembourg, Malaysia, Netherlands, New Zealand, Norway, Papua New Guinea, Saint Kitts and Nevis, Saint Lucia, Saint Vincent and the Grenadines, Solomon Islands, Spain, Sweden, Thailand, Tonga, Tuvalu, United Kingdom.

A Republic, with Executive Head of State, Presidency Independent of Legislature and Ministry being subjected to parliamentary confidence.

Algeria, Burkina Faso, Côte d' Ivories, Democratic Republic of the Congo, Djibouti, France, Georgia, Guinea-Bissau, Guyana, Haiti, Kenya, Kyrgyzstan, Lithuania, Madagascar, Mali, Mauritania, Mongolia, Niger, Palestine, Portugal, Romania, Russia, Sâo Tomé and Principe, Senegal, Sri Lanka, Republic of China (Taiwan), Tajikistan.

A Republic, with Executive Head of State, Presidency, And Ministry are subjected to parliamentary confidence.

Botswana, Marshall Islands, Nauru, South Africa,

Monarch personally exercises power in concert with other institutions.

Bahrain, Bhutan, Jordan, Kuwait, Liechtenstein, Monaco, United Arab Emirates.

Power constitutionally linked to a single political movement.

Cuba, Eritrea, Laos, Libya, North Korea, People's Republic of China, Sahrawi Republic, Syria, Turkmenistan.

All authority vested in absolute monarch

Brunei, Qatar, Swaziland, Vatican City.

All authority vested in current monarch
Oman and Saudi Arabia.

Somalia has become a stateless society.
Egypt and Fiji have no constitutionally –
defined basis to current regime.

☐ ☐ ☐ ☐ ☐

We shall now look at the various **ideologies** practiced by
countries currently involved in Libya's civil wars?

Democracy (Practiced in the Western nations.)
Democracy is the best system of governance in Africa.
Without it, you would have civil wars, and insecurity.
Democracy has worked in some African countries like
Ghana, Cape Verde, Botswana, South Africa, Tanzania,
The Gambia, and others. But my natural analytical instinct tells
me that history could have influenced these outcomes. You see
there had been real controls enforced by the Afrikaans, the
Dutch, the Ruthless dictators like General Smuts, and their
apartheid regimes (a policy of racial segregation and political
and economic discrimination against non-Europeans groups in
the Republic of So. Africa.)
Majorities of blacks yielded like voiceless, gutless slaves. Nelson
Mandela, who rebelled against the system, was imprisoned for
most of his adult life. This resulted in a generation of

32

uneducated masses with "Let it be!" mentality who would accept any and all circumstance, unlike the modern and rebellious youth.

To sustain democracy, one has to engage in civic education at individual, community and national levels continuously. Policies and programs for the maintenance of democracy and good governance must be strictly followed, and a system of checks and balances must be adhered to religiously. This was not the case during the Apartheid era.

Libya was a unique state under a dictator, who could glue together widely split Muslim tribes under a

SINGLE POLITICAL MOVEMENT.

It was indeed a case of uniting the uneducated, disjointed masses under a commander, to fight a common enemy-

i.e. (USA!) They were virtually trained, and were psyched under a *FEAR & HATE COMPLEX.*

Gaddafi established a unique system of communist form of control for all possessions like homes, vehicles, and centralized all weapons in secret underground cells under 24x7 vigilance. His propaganda machine brainwashed Libyans to think that he is the Big Brother, protecting them from evil foreigners.

All in all the system of sharing some of the wealth under the Jamahiriya, kept poverty, underdevelopment of children, and lack of food for nourishment out.

Communism vs. Capitalism and Democracy

Differences between these three are not absolute, nor clear cut but I enlist some definitions here any way.

Democracy is based on the principal of equality and freedom. Certain liberties are protected under the constitution. It is a political system of governance preferably carried out by the elected representatives.

There is no nation that has adopted the original true communism as defined by Karl Marx, who created this ideology.

Russia and China who started some form of Communism have changed over to their own special mixture of Communism and Socialism and are quickly finding comfort in a mixture of Democratic capitalism.

Communism really is an *socio-economic* system for the establishment of a classless, egalitarian and stateless society. It is more of an economic concept rather than a political one. Most countries rejected it, because of its violent nature. Communism became virtually a POLICE Estate, having secret police like Gestapo, in the practicing countries.
In Libya the Green Beret was the equivalent of Gestapo.

Capitalism works when it is well controlled by the Government. Left to itself it rots to the "banker level," who collect your money and pay you some interest and sell it back to you for your needs for large item purchases at very high interest rates. They make lots of profit-called Margin or Leverage in the process. This was going on for years, till the public in Western Countries, completely lost the habit of Savings for the rainy day.

They were thus hooked on to "Borrowing," "Loans" not only for their daily needs such as Homes, Education of their kids, Cars, Luxury items etc, but with the advent of a pocket-able plastic device called the *CREDIT CARD* they were truly enslaved, to over extending their credit limits. These cards were the easy way to empower them to fulfil their dependency on drugs, illicit sex, and every member of each family could use this evil convenience and were also had the freedom to misuse them if they wanted, without realizing or thinking of the unintended consequences.

Government helped, by facilitating loans for the educational necessities, not realizing that these easy to get tools could be misused, by the cardholder. Parents of these kids, followed by the Government were subjected to very high debts plus the compounding interest on them.

The Housing industry, the Commercial Houses, the Sears, the Safeway, the Wall Marts of the world and the several other retail industries were flooded with clever techniques and derivatives to tempt the innocent borrowers with loans for things they could live without. The homebuilders came up with new colonies of beautiful homes, which were sold, before you could see, touch or feel them, Viz., when they were on the drawing board. The banks gave them loans, without checking their capacity to pay, and the appraisers raised their values without limits. The security deposited for the mortgages was the free air, because the construction and completion were years into the future. The maximum down payment for the first buyer was about 5%. I actually bought and resold my paper contract in Houston, and made lot of cash profit in those days. The oil companies used their lobbyist to kill any plans to develop public transportation. This encouraged the easy way out, of having a car and a garage for each member of every family, who then borrowed money for all those vehicles, without any means to pay for the monthly notes. The credit

35

cards were a misnomer, and attracted penalties and charges for late fees.

The debt kept on building, till it reached ballooning proportions. This resulted in the present stalemate between the Republicans, and Democrats, and the formation of the *THE NEW TEA PARTY MOVEMENT!* insists on reducing the size of the Government, needed to administer capitalism. They also want Obama to limit borrowing and reduce spending. This at best could result in changing the party in power. But like the Bush Administration, they will go all hog in spending even more than the present Government and raise (not lower) the debt, till the next elections 4 years hence, when the pendulum would swing in favor of the only other party and so on. There is no solution unless a strong third party is established.

We can go on endlessly describing the evils of the Capitalist. Very soon people like Madeoff came on the horizon with their Ponzie schemes, robbing millions from the very people who were held in great esteem by their own religious (Jews) leaders.

Madeoff-made off with total wealth of Mr. Sinking. Also Michael Milken was milking the stock market through his trashy Junk Bonds.

As rightly explained by B. Jaykrishnan in response to *"POST RECESSION ENLIGHTENMENT,"* we saw men and women with zero ethics toppling the world with financial **Kalashnikovs** called derivatives?

The real capitalist society in the *USA* politics today is *the TEA PARTY.* It is openly claiming that all the woes of our economy are the oversized Government and the taxes they demand from the multimillionaires. The richest are too smart to pay them. They would find loopholes and move money outside the country, rather than follow the tax collectors' laws, because they are foxy, and do not intend to part with their hard-earned wealth, to be used by the

Government for expenses and earmarked programs!

Thus USA politics have two parties. One makes lot of money the Capitalists Way-i.e. Earns it. The other is the Democratic Party who believes in the Socialist Democratic system of Government controls, Taxes, and Unions. They encourage the Social Security System.

We can go on, but as readers know, there is no one solution that is the best, for all circumstances, in every country, all the time, to follow.

Thus ideologies followed by different countries, listed earlier are liable to change. Libya's present governance would change because it is simply geared to getting rid of Gaddafi as a common enemy of the rebels and the western world but for different reasons.

So far it is a melting pot, with uncertain future?

There will have to be rigid and iron discipline before we achieve anything great and enduring, and that discipline will not come by mere academic argument and appeal to reason and logic. Discipline is learnt in the school of adversity.

Mahatma Gandhi

*Man must understand that when he cuts himself
from all stimulating and purifying
Contact with infinity and no longer relies on it for his
subsistence and his health.
He Risks madness; he tears himself asunder, and divorces
himself from his very substance*

Rabindranath
Tagore

THOUGH IT MAY TAKE VARIOUS ROADS, ALL ARE ON THE WAY.

Swami Vivekananda.

— — —

*Truth resides in the heart of every man.
And it is there he must seek it, in order to be guided by it
so that, at the least, it will appear to him.
But we do not have the right to force others
to see the Truth in our way.*

Mahatma Gandhi

LIBYA
UNDER MUAMMAR GADDAFI
1969–2011

His Zodiac Sign! *Born in June 1942,* - (These people born under the Gemini sign tend to cut corners. They are a little more convincing in order to reach goals closer to their heart.)

He ruled for *42 years* *starting from* *1969*. *He was* *69 years old, when he was killed.*

On 1 September 1969, a small group of military officers led by 27-year-old army officer Muammar Gaddafi staged a coup d'état against King Idris, launching the Libyan Revolution. Gaddafi was referred to as the "Brother Leader and Guide of the Revolution" in government statements and the official Libyan press.

Gaddafi was a great admirer of the Nasser regime in Egypt and had negotiated a Joint army and Airforce deal between the two neighboring countries.

After Nasser's death, Gaddafi attempted to become a leader of Arab Nationalism. He wanted to unify the Arab states of North Africa into a "Great Islamic State of the Sahel." In 1969 he contributed to the Islamization of Sudan and Chad, granting military bases and support to the FROLINAT revolutionary forces. In 1971 when Muslims took power in Sudan, he offered to merge Libya with Sudan. After Jaafar Nimiery turned him down he took matters into his own hands and organized a paramilitary group in 1972, to Arabize the region. He dispatched The Islamic Legion to Lebanon, Syria, Uganda, and Palestine, to take active measures in establishing Islamic control. He encouraged young students to join the Libyan Volunteer Army.

He convinced Anwar Sadat to join Egypt and Libya under a common Flag over which Sadat will preside and Gaddafi will become a defense Minister. Sadat distrusted Gaddafi, and had no knowledge of Libyan military planes secretly joining the Egyptian Air Force in 1973. Also the outbreak of the Yom Kippur War surprised Gaddafi, as Egypt and Syria planned it without his knowledge. Gaddafi rightfully felt this attempt with a limited objective as a waste of human and military resources, and weakening the FAR. Libya's relations with Egypt further weakened, when Sadat spearheaded the peace talks with Israel under the American leadership. Gaddafi called Sadat a coward for pussyfooting after a counteroffensive by Israel. Sadat was quick to blame Gaddafi for the foiling of a 1973 submarine attack when Libya was supposed to sink the RMS Queen Elizabeth 2 during an Israel cruise. Gaddafi fired back saying the Arabs could have destroyed Israel within 12 hours if they had adopted a sound strategy. He said that Sadat had no control of Egyptian information media. Egypt's peace talks in 1977 led to the Steadfastness and Confrontation Front, a group

Gaddafi formed to reject the recognition of the Israel State. Complete breakdown of Egypt-Libyan relations resulted in a short-lived war between them. Gaddafi applauded Sadat's assassination in October 1981, calling it as a punishment for his role in Camp David Accords. From time to time he responded to external opposition, with violence.

Later that same year, Gaddafi ordered an artillery strike on Egypt in retaliation against Egyptian President Anwar Sadat's intent to sign a peace treaty with Israel.

Sadat's forces triumphed easily in a four-day border war that came to be known as the Libyan-Egyptian War, leaving over 400 Libyans dead and Gaddafi's armored divisions in disarray.

On the birthday of the Prophet Muhammad in 1973, Gaddafi delivered a "Five-Point Address."

He announced the suspension of all existing laws and replaced them by a Sheria Law. He said that the country would be purged of the "politically sick." A "People's Militia" would "protect the revolution".

After the 1969 coup, Muammar Gaddafi closed American and British bases and partly nationalized foreign oil and commercial interests in Libya.

Gaddafi was known for backing a number of leaders viewed as anathema *to Westernization and political liberalism, including Ugandan President Idi Amin, Central African Emperor Jean-Bedel Bokassa, Ethiopian strongman Haile Mariam Mengistu, Liberian President Charles Taylor, and Yugoslav President Slobodan Milošević.*
Relations with the West were strained by a series of incidents during
most of Gaddafi's rule. These included but were not limited to the:

41

Killing of British policewoman Yvonne Fletcher.

Bombing of a Berlin nightclub frequented by U.S. servicemen, and of Pan Am Flight 103, which led to UN sanctions in the 1990s.

Though by the late 2000s, the United States and other Western powers had normalized relations with Libya.

Gaddafi's decision to abandon the pursuit of weapons of mass destruction after the Iraq War saw Iraqi dictator Saddam Hussein overthrown and put on trial led to Libya being hailed as a success for Western soft power initiatives in the War on Terror.

Gaddafi in his first UN appearance on Wednesday Sept.23, 2009, *ISSUED A SCATHING ATTACK* on the Security Council and chastised the world body for failing to intervene or prevent some 65 wars since its founding in 1945.

His speech followed President Barrack Obama's first General Assembly address. U.S. Secretary of State Hillary Rodham Clinton and US Ambassador Susan Rice departed before Gaddafi ascended the podium.

However on the opposite side her counter part, the Secretary of State in Bush's presidency, Condoleezza Rice, was very friendly and visited his abode in Sirte personally. Judged by the album found in his personal drawers and her interview with Piers Morgan they were completely amicable. As a result Gaddafi gave several millions of dollars to the families of the victims of the *PAN AM* flight, a far cry from Hillary's behavior!

As Gaddafi addressed the General assembly demonstrators protested Scotland's recent release of Libyan Abdel Baset al-Megrahi who was convicted of the 1988 bombing of Pan Am Flight 103 which killed 270 innocent people. It was ever so depressing for me because one of our family friends in Torrance was also killed. Mr Bhatia's death was hurtful because he never came back to his wife and daughter, who we see often and they lost their loved one for no rhyme or reason. Thanks to Rice, my friend received 10 million dollars in compensation.

In May 2010, Libya was elected by the UN General Assembly to a three-year term on the UN's Human Rights Council. It was subsequently suspended from the Human Rights Council in March 2011.

Gaddafi set up an extensive surveillance system. Ten to Twenty percent of Libyans work in surveillance for the Revolutionary committees. The surveillance takes place in government, in factories, and in the education sector.

I can not forget the case of my own Lebanese contractor who was unaware that he was to be hanged in a public square, because of his breaching a canon of the Shería Law. He gave the much-needed loan to his worker for which he got lots of gratification. But because he received an interest on that money he was to be taught a lesson-viz., hanged till he dies! I am given high regards by the Lebanese community in Beverly hill for my helping him cross over to the Chad border overnight and helping his family in their dire needs.

In another incidence I was stopped in public and a low ranking lavatory cleaner, was ready to smash the windscreen of my car. His grouse was that I put the phone down on him when he called me. I have no idea what when and how I had done that, because I never had direct dealings with, nor time for him or his bosses in my executive position. This case is unbelievable and cannot be visualized in any other country or circumstances! But the reason was obvious. Here he had the secret support of the supreme commander of Libya!

The case of undermining the direct authority of a superior in the presence of his workers is counter disciplinarian if you ask me!

I can relate several cases but the number of pages would be prohibitive. However here is one case that boggles my mind to this day. I was conducting an urgent meeting with my 49 British and European engineers.

When I pressed the button under my rosewood table in the Boardroom, my British secretary appeared. I asked her to "Xerox" for me a copy of the statement; I handed over to her. A few minutes, after she left, I was facing two military personnel who barged into the Boardroom and put a gun on my neck in front of all my subordinates and asked me to produce my *PASSPORT*, which we had to carry all the time on our body.

Later I discovered that I was treated shabbily because a senior ranking officer like me involved with a Jewish Company like *XEROX*, cannot be tolerated!

To this day, I do not know if Xerox was a Jewish Company or using the operative word "Xerox"- shows my involvement with that Jewish Company?

Anyhow all future copying machines were ordered from a low ranking European company, and they were, *A DEAD LOSS*!

Gaddafi executed dissidents publicly and the executions were often rebroadcast on state television channels.

Gaddafi employed his network of diplomats and recruits to assassinate dozens of critical refugees around the world.

Amnesty International listed at least 25 assassinations between 1980 and 1987.

In 1977, Libya officially became the "Socialist People's Libyan Arab Jamahiriya."

Gaddafi officially passed power to the General People's Committees and henceforth claimed to be no more than a symbolic figurehead, but domestic and international critics claimed the reforms gave him virtually unlimited power. He told me that he had decided to give himself the title of a Col., because he wanted to associate himself as a popular "One of them guys in the streets or foot soldiers in the military!"

Dissidents against the new system were not tolerated. Gaddafi himself authorized punitive actions including capital punishment. The new Jamahiriya governance structure he established was officially referred to as a form of direct democracy. Though the government refused to publish election results.

Gaddafi called Chirac, offering help in quelling the resistors, who were largely North African.

Following a 1986-aborted attempt to replace English with Russian as the primary foreign language in education, students continued to have access to English level media. However one protester in 2011 said that: "None of us can speak English or French. He kept us ignorant and blindfolded."

In 1986 the United States sought to quell Libya's alleged terrorist activities by bombing several sites in Libya. Gaddafi once told me that Reagan, the great President of a great country, does not have the capability of judging the big tactical mistake he is making, by giving a small country like Libya an undue importance. "This is good for me!" Gaddafi uttered, "Because I get free publicity and a raise in my international fame." However Western media have since speculated that Gaddafi suffers from manic depression, schizophrenia, and megalomania. I refused to believe this even in my dreams or ever dare show a hint of it on my face, whenever I was up close to him!

Anwar Sadat called him "unbalanced and immature" and a "vicious criminal." Gaafar Nimiery called him an "evil" person, and Yasser Arafat, who aligned himself with Gaddafi for much of his career, said Gaddafi was the "knight of revolutionary phrases." Fidel Castro said he was "reckless." In February 1977, Libya started delivering military supplies to Goukouni Oueddei and the People's Armed Forces in Chad. The Chadian–Libyan conflict began in earnest when Libya's support of rebel forces in northern Chad escalated into an invasion. I remember when we were returning from a trip after jet cleaning the heavy dessert sand deposits on the insulator trees of the

High Tension Overhead lines, at 4 am college girls were marching with heavy rifles on their shoulders near Bengazi. They were on their way to be transported to the Chad warfront.

Later we discovered that these college students were taken out straight from their colleges, and were sent to the war front with no bullets in their rifles, and had zero war experiences. Some of those who survived came back with one or more limbs lost!

Hundreds of Libyans lost their lives in the war against Tanzania, when Gaddafi tried to save his friend Idi Amin. Indian and Pakistanis, citizens in Amin country, hated him. Every one called him a MADMAN.

Gaddafi financed various other groups varying from anti-nuclear movements to Australian trade unions.

From 1977 onward, per capita income in the country rose to more than US $11,000, the fifth-highest in Africa, while the Human Development Index became the highest in Africa and greater than that of Saudi Arabia.

This was achieved without borrowing any foreign loans, and keeping Libya debt-free.

He decentralized the ruling Junta! Tripoli is sometimes referred to as the de-facto capital of Libya, since none of the country's ministries were located there. Even the National General People's Congress was held annually in Sirte -the birthplace of Col. Gaddafi.

As part of a radical decentralization program undertaken on September 1988 all General People's secretariats (ministries,) except those responsible for foreign liaison (foreign affairs) and information, were located away from Tripoli. The former Secretariat for Economy was moved to Benghazi and Health ministry to Kufra. In 1993 secretariat for Foreign Liaison and International Co-operation was being moved to Ras Lanouf.

Gaddafi had an A1 (Alpha Male) personality, graciously generous to his followers, admirers, and loyalist army, but a vicious, ruthless, marauder to those who opposed him. He was capable of using torture techniques worse than those used in the days of Spanish Inquisition.

Col. Gaddafi was a unique man, with unique characteristics and possessed an unparalleled, matchless personality.

He was a madman to some, especially those who were mad at him.

He had that rare in-born ability and that special twist of mind, a poker face to conceal the true quality of his hand (in poker.)

If you ever claim, that you can truly judge this unique character, you would need the ability to have an expressionless face to start with.

Most importantly you must be up-close and live around him for over a year to decipher his sharp wit, foxy characteristics and mastermind. He was a man of few words and they differed considerably depending on his mood and the strength with which he kicked his fists up in the air.

Gaddafi's name to fame as the world's most notorious guy took place during the last 20 of his 42 years of reign!

I was posted for 3 years as an *EXXON* executive staff in the early eighties.

After the burning of the American Embassy, and the departure of hundreds of Americans, including my family, I was asked to stay on.in Libya, because Exxon did not want to leave their billion dollar facilities, in the hands of Libyans.

I was most needed, because Gaddafi happened to respect me as his Indian professor-look-alike. Exxon appreciated my timely presence and help and catapulted me to the second in command, next to a high level Exxon executive from Canada. *With the close association with the Reagan Administration and Gaddafi I was in a critically sensitive and dangerous situation to say the least!*

An airstrike failed to kill Gaddafi in 1986. Several other attempts on his life including poisoning him when he was hospitalized failed. In that particular incidence the nurse who was planted to do the job fell in love with him and warned him about the plan set by the *CIA*

After the bombing of a commercial flight killing hundreds of travelers, Libya was put under United Nations sanctions

Gaddafi assumed the honorific title of "King of Kings of Africa" in 2008. The early 2010s, in addition to attempting to assume a leadership role in the African Union, also viewed Libya as having formed closer ties with Italy, one of its former colonial rulers, compared to any other country in the European Union. Gaddafi had a high percentage ownership of the FIAT corporation as a stock holder.

Under former Prime Ministers Shukri Ghanem and Baghdad Mahmudi, Libya underwent a business boom, *with initiatives to privatize many government-run industries. Many international oil companies returned to the country, including oil giants Shell and ExxonMobil.*

Tourism was on the rise, bringing increased demand for hotel accommodation and for capacity at airports such as Tripoli International.

A multi-million dollar renovation of Libyan airports was approved in 2006 by the government to help meet such demands.

According to the Economist magazine, the eastern parts of the country have been 'ruined' due to Gaddafi's economic theories, Libya has enjoyed a low level of both absolute and relative poverty. In the first six years of the new millennium Libyan officials of the Libyan Arab Jamahiriya era carried out economic reforms as part of a broader campaign to reintegrate the country into the global capitalist economy.

This effort picked up steam after UN sanctions were lifted in September 2003 after Libya announced in December 2003 that it would abandon programs to build weapons of mass destruction.

Authorities had privatized more than 100 government owned companies since 2003 in industries, including oil refining, tourism and real estate, of which 29 are 100% foreign, owned.

In addition, financial support was provided for university scholarships and employment programs.

Life expectancy rose from 57 to 77 years, equal rights were established for women and black people.

Employment opportunities were established for migrant workers, and welfare systems were introduced that allowed access to free education, free healthcare, and financial assistance for housing. The Great Manmade River was also built to allow free access to fresh water across large parts of the country.

{Above information has been taken from Wikipedia}

Much of the country's income from oil, which soared in the 1970s, was spent on arms purchases and on sponsoring dozens of paramilitaries and terrorist groups around the world.

The non-oil manufacturing and construction sectors, which account for about 20% of G D P, were expanded from processing mostly agricultural products to include the production of petrochemicals, iron, steel, and aluminum.

Climatic conditions and poor soils severely limit agricultural output, and Libya imports about 75% of its food.

Water was also a problem, with some 28% of the population not having access to safe drinking water in 2000.

The Great Manmade River project tapped into vast underground aquifers of fresh water discovered during the quest for oil, and was intended to improve the country's agricultural output.

Gaddafi was afraid that the students or their parents would revolt at any time. So he arranged that people stay far from each other. He created a big separation in the maps between East and West Libya-a vast, impenetrable desert-to disorient people and make sure they felt divided, not united. School books (particularly on Geography) and Maps were designed to confuse the users, rather than inform them.

He ensured that the most vital (a must) subject taught was the Al Mujtama Al- Jamahiriya, the study of "Green Book"- Gaddafi's core treatise on politics and civic life.

His Green Book (1980) is a treatise on Islamic Socialism. He professes it as a "Third Universe Theory."

The Democracy as described in this book is the supervision of the people directly by the people and not by "popular expressions."

There are no political parties, classes, or institutions of power, which claim to represent the people or to dominate the masses of people in any way.

He used to argue bitterly against my claim that USA is a democracy and India is the largest of all democracies. He insisted that in his experience the Police and the Mayors *MISUSED THEIR AUTHORITY,* especially in smaller USA towns. Information about molestation of little innocent kids and other foul plays, by people in power are always suppressed (even in Churches.)

In most movies the *BAD COPS* are always the forces to reckon with until the end of the movie.

Frankly *GREEN BOOK* is a hotchpotch of populism, socialism, and a stateless world run by liberated masses. A grand product of his political vision, now that he has reached a Nirvana stage. It all started with his taking over the radio and television broadcasting stations in Benghazi in September 1969.

That is when he announced to Libya and the world, that he had overthrown King Idris Sanussi.

That also was the start of the Al Fateh Revolution-

During his *FLASH CRASH* at the Brega families Recreational Club, he insisted that I read, analyze, and discuss this book. I gave him a dose of Hindu Philosophy, and Sanskrit scriptures instead.

He sent a letter of congratulations to Obama, praising him on his election in 2008, but later referred to him as his "African son who wants to kill me." He criticized America for not having free healthcare and free education.

"THE ERA OF THE MASSES."

Today the grand nephew of Idris Sanussi, Mohammed El Senussi, considered by his Libyan royalists to be the heir to the old Libyan throne said that the flag of freedom is flying in Sirte and across Libya.

It took 8 months for the rebels with air cover by the mighty western nations, and unlimited supply of arms to every young and old to bring down Gaddafi, whose prowess took only 8 minutes to dethrone the old king.

He was defiant till the end. He vowed for "Death or Victory." He did not run away in fear. *He did not brutalize the King after dethroning him, yet he received the most brutal end, and was subjected to Sodomy.* It is a Shame. Such an ugly end has never been meted out even to a rat, any derelict, despots, or anyone's worst enemy that I have ever come across?

It is a telltale sign and a classic example of the lowest evil humans who may become the next rulers of Libya, notwithstanding the fact that Gaddafi was a ruthless dictator, who tortured his enemies with vengeance.

Now it is being reported that Anti-Gaddafi forces have executed 53 Gaddafi loyalists, which causes one to wonder if the new government will truly bring freedom and democracy to Libya.

Most are concerned that another Dictator will replace the Dictator and the bloodshed will not end soon.

The human voice can never reach the distance
That is covered by the small voice of conscience.

Mahatma Gandi.

Find the Unique and possess the Whole.
This truly is our highest, most sublime privilege.
It is in the law of this unity that is, as long as we understand it,
Our immutable force. Its living principle is the force that resides in
truth___Truth is one.

Rabindranath Tagore

The Outward freedom that we shall attain wil
only be in exact proportion to the Inward freedom
to which we may have grown ay any given moment

Mahatma Gandhi

LAST EIGHT MONTHS OF GADDAFI'S POWER STRUGGLE!

His supporters had several clashes with the rebels for eight months after the start of the "Arab Spring" revolt.
He also rewarded his loyalists with free-living quarters, TVs, telephones, and transport!

He was a deadly leader, and master of counter-espionage. He suffered from delirium, and became helpless, after his sovereign Air Power was crushed by heavy bombardment of tomahawks and rebels were crawling all over his personal property and his secret tunnels! He was brought down to the level of a slave, as compared to a declared King at the African Summit, in less than a year. Earlier he used all his fighting power to crush the revolt. He killed the commander of rebel forces and accentuated his propaganda machine.

His counterespionage abilities had been honed by frontline experience over 42 years (some fatal).

He trusted **no one.**

He started ruling Libya from 1969 and he was 69 years old when he was reportedly hiding in a drainpipe (like his friend Saddam Hussain of Iraq,) on October 20, 2011. THAT DAY WILL GO IN LIBYAN HISTORY AS

V G R

(VICTORY OVER GADDAFI's REGIME)

For a super sharp guy as I knew him this state of helplessness had reached because of the Superior technology of the Satellites, Google maps, and Drones. After all these tools were responsible for throwing Assama Bin Laden to the sharks in deep blue seas. His truck was located with pinpoint accuracy and Gaddafi was virtually handed over to the vicious rebels on a platter. He was alive and bleeding, when he was captured. I saw the mobile phone footage of him being subjected to sodomy, and his body being dragged through the streets of his neighboring palatial residence. The scenes were so graphically obnoxiously that it would be suffice to say that a cat would drag a dead rat a little more tenderly!

On September 2009, he was delivering a scathing attack on the Security Council during his U. N. appearance. He wore Bedouin robes and had a black pin shaped like Africa decorating his heart. He censured the world body for their inability to intervene in or preventing some 65 wars since it was founded in 1945!

He attended the G-8 summit in 2009, where he was honored and seated next to President Obama!

Major political protests began in Libya against Gaddafi's government on February 17, 2011.

His violent response to the protests prompted defections from his government. Gaddafi accused the rebels of being "drugged" and linked to Al-Qaeda. Reports in press hinted of his hiring Ghanian mercenaries @ $2500 per day. Advertisements for this appeared in Nigerian newspapers. He communicated with Ukranian and Serbian mercenaries in Belarus. His son's Khamis Brigade went into full-fledged action creating havoc and imposing brutalities to the revolting civilians. *A NATO HELICOPTER WAS SHOT DOWN, AND BREGA WAS LIBERATED THAT DAY!*

At his testimony on Capitol Hill, Defense Secretary Robert Gates, pleaded against another exercise in nation building. He considered the *"NO FLY ZONE,"* -an act of war, because after all you are forcing Gaddafi out of his own sovereign airspace! Bombarding that space using *NATO* and Western airpowers to kill Gaddafi and supporting the untrained civilians with air cover. He was hoping Gaddafi loyalists would turn against him, if smart diplomacy could convert them.

On the other hand Leon Panetta used the Superior Drones and tools of modern scientific development to kill Assama- Bin-Laadan, and Gaddafi quietly and remotely.

Every person old, young male, females were provided with guns and innumerable bullets. The bullets were being sprayed, just for the sake of making a political statement, showing presence and *BROADCASTING A SHOW OF AUTHORITY*. Most of the targets were missed. Everyone had a *FUN PARTY*, especially on his sprawling private residential compound in Sirte, soon after the pounding by NATO's

tomahawks (million dollars a piece for each Bomb alone!)
Everyone behaved like an illiterate and a vagrant kid!
Now those armaments and dangerous weapons are accessible
to the evil forces and the opportunists of the future. These
ticking bombs, and the caches abandoned by the regime and
subsequently looted, highlight the scope of escalating strife,
inside the country, as well as in the wider region.
These include shoulder-launched surface-to-air missiles.
Known as Manpads, capable of bringing down commercial
airlines.
The uncontrolled proliferation of this largest stockpile of
Manpads- these portable defense systems, as well as munitions
and mines, has become a potential risk to the local and regional
stability. The continuing human rights abuses are the most
pressing concerns of the *NTC*.

Over 7000 Political prisoners, released by the Gaddafi regime
are currently held in makeshift detention centers, under the
control of the revolutionary brigade with no access to due
process, in the absence of functioning police and judiciary.
Of particular worry is the fate of women being held for alleged
links with the defunct regime, often due to family connections,
sometimes with their children locked up alongside them, under
male supervision.
A group of black Africans were lynched following the
revolution, as they were falsely accused of being hired guns
during Gaddafi regime.
The port city of Tawerga suffered prolonged and brutal siege at
the hands of regime and was largely destroyed by rebel fighters,
primarily because they were suspected of being mercenaries.
They were detained in large numbers and subjected to torture
and ill treatment. Individuals have been targeted for the color
of their skin. It is a jungle out there.
Tawergas have been the victims of revenge killings, and taken
from their homes, checkpoints and hospitals by armed men,

and subsequently abused or executed in detention. The Gaddafi regime also detained civilians in agricultural warehouses, during the final days of the civil war as reported by Ban Ki-Moon, in the UN finding chart. Some were tortured and massacred. He laid misery over Misreta.

In syria conditions are worst but no one is bothered, since they have no oil to offer? it is free for all and west does not care, as long as, the oil flows.

In August 2011, Ahmed Jehani, head of the Libyan Stabilization Team appointed by the rebel National Transition Council, estimated it would take at least **10 years** to rebuild Libya's infrastructure.

He also noted that Libya's infrastructure was in a poor state, even before the 2011 civil war due to "utter neglect" by Gaddafi's administration.

Ninety percent of the people live in less than 10% of the area, primarily along the coast.

About 88% of the population are urban, mostly concentrated in three largest cities, Tripoli, Benghazi and Misrata. Libya has a population of about 6.5 million, around half of whom are under the age of 15. In 1984 the population reached 3.6 million and was growing about 4% a year, one of the highest rates in the world.

There would be an administrative revolution, and a Cultural Revolution. Libya's human rights record was put in the spotlight in February 2011, due to the government's violent response to pro-democracy protesters, when it killed hundreds of demonstrators.

In 2011, Freedom House rated both political rights and civil liberties in Libya as "7" (1 representing the most free and 7 the least free rating), and gave it the freedom rating of "Not Free." Compared to its neighbors.

Tens of thousands of people in Libya are waiting to cross the border into Tunisia, after clashes between Libyan Mercenary Forces and protesters, left hundreds dead.

Libyans frustrated by the rule of de-facto leader Muammar Gaddafi have followed in the footsteps of Tunisia and Egypt, taking to the streets in the hope the controversial figure's tenure can be ended.

But their hopes of a peaceful transition were dashed when Gaddafi's forces unleashed a wave of violence, sending the country into panic.

National Transitional Council militiamen deployed a three-car convoy into Bani Walid only for it to be destroyed in an ambush that claimed at least four NTC fighters. Fighting is also raging near Sirte. Dr. Alsharif who heads a field hospital near the city, said that at least 80 NTC fighters had been killed there since Saturday. NATO warplanes have repeatedly blitzed the defenders' positions. But the main NTC milita was forced into a headlong retreat from Bani Walid on Friday. Now the frontline is made up of bands of undisciplined rag tag fighters.

Western journalists reported that NTC –allied fighters as young as 18 were spending hours smoking cannabis, shooting at plastic bottles, arguing with one another and sometimes just firing wildly into the streets out of apparent boredom.

In Benghazi today NTC chief Mahmoud Jibril told a press conference that the council had failed to reach an agreement on an interim government due to bickering over positions.

On Sunday Gaddafi partisans had captured 17 mercenaries including fighters from Britain, France and Qatar.

Now, the Libya-Tunisia border area and passport processing zone has been overwhelmed by people wishing to leave the country urgently - many have been desperately waiting in this particular area for days.

The conflict has put enormous strain on the already volatile North African region - and the effects will be far reaching. The UN has said that the Tunisian-Libyan border situation has reached "crisis point."

The UN is also urging co-operation of governments to undertake a "massive humanitarian evacuation of tens of thousands of Egyptians and other third country nationals." A large number of Tuaregs immigrated to Libya from Mali and Niger to serve as mercenaries in Libyan leader Muammar Gaddafi's army. Now, dozens of families living in Libya are preparing to do the opposite and return to their homeland. According to the UN's International Organization for Migration, border crossings between Libya and Niger have surged since the start of the unrest. Eighteen hundred of the 2,205 people, who entered Niger on March 10, were native Nigerians.

The UN estimates that 60,000 more people may arrive in Niger from Libya in the next few weeks.

It was rumored that Aisha Gaddhafi may seek Asylum in Israel? That surely cannot be true? Gadhafi's soul will become restless in misery.

What a turncoat she is after her father spent all his life and guts
going after the Jews! Even I was taken to the cleaners, when
they took me to the military court at gunpoint, for uttering a
word "Xerox" to my British secretary, asking her to make a
copy!
NATO started as a political association. Now it has become a
military wing of the intergovernmental alliance. They have been
involved in full-fledged wars in three continents, for the past 12
years, starting with the fall of the Berlin Wall in 1989.
President George W. Bush set up the AFRICOM (United
States–Africa Command) in 2008, after demitting office. The
demand for a permanent American footprint on the African
continent had come from the right-wing think tanks that
enjoyed great clout in the corridors of power
During Gaddafi's reign, there were no interest on loans-if some
made a blunder in charging an iota of interest he would be
hanged in the public square and that event would be televised
and broadcast to act as a deterrent. Electricity was free for all
citizens. Banks were state-owned and loans were given at 0%
interest per Sheria law.

Tripoli fell, and Gaddafi is in hiding, trying to turn
Libya into true hell. A top US envoy brought best
wishes, but no Humvees or blast barriers- nor any
blueprints for rebuilding a nation. The political process
is frenzied and bewildering; hosts of gun trucks and
Kalashnikovs are roaring away, yet there are no foreign
troops on the ground.

Tripoli has become a kind of anti-Baghdad, in one aspect.

Nothing like the chilling, ambush-prone roadblocks
long manned by edgy U.S. troops in Baghdad, or any
trunk loads of hundred dollar bills to help rebuild
Tripoli.

LIBYA'S UNREST:

(DEFIANT GADDAFI VOWS DEATH OR VICTORY)

Col. Muammar Gadddafi has made a speech vowing death or
victory in the fight against "aggression,"
After Libyan rebels seized his Tripoli compound.
He declared that he had made a "tactical" retreat from his Bab
al-Aziziya compound in the capital.
Is it a real or a false threat?

The compound was not taken by a victory in a genuine
war. It was found vacated and while they were looking
for the leader, who disappeared mysteriously, they were
ransacking all his personal belongings! They were
relishing their symbolic control over him through his
personal possessions. Perhaps imagining that they are
crushing his head under the sole of their dirty shoes. He
is hopelessly helpless. This was the virtual outburst of
their anger and frustration caused by his devilish
treatment of their loved ones in the past.

Their anger turned into Shock and Awe when as they
probed, deeper into the sub tunnels and hideouts
underground. They had to hand carry and remove his
large and defaced portraits in the compound, which had
already been pounded by rockets and bombs.

The carnage and chaos led them to an area, smelling of powerful stink arising from an underground warehouse, full of horror, where they came across the bones and charred remains of 50 dead bodies. These were allegedly massacred and mutilated by the dreaded Khamis Brigade, commandeered by his young son.

They sifted through family photos and files. It is not difficult to imagine how upset and mad Gaddafi must be feeling, seeing and finding how the people who were scared to death by his name are now entering and mutilating his family's personal possessions! One picture shows a rebel fighter resting his dirty shoes on the head of Aisha Gaddafi's gilded mermaid and her clean sofa! Gaddafi's violent response to the protestors prompted defection from his government. His number two man A.F.Younis, Mustafa Abdel-Jalil and several key ambassadors and diplomats resigned from their posts in protest. Other government officials refused to follow his orders and were jailed for insubordination. By late February the country was rapidly descending into chaos. The government had lost control of Eastern Libya. Gaddafi fought back declaring that rebels have been drugged and Saudi Arabia's al-Qaida terror group had moved in! At the beginning of March 2011 Gaddafi returned from hideout, relying on considerable amount of Libyan and US$ cash *THAT HAD APPARENTLY BEEN STASHED IN THE CAPITAL!*

A NATO air strike killed Gaddafi's youngest son and his grandsons at his son's Tripoli home on April 30. Government officials said that Gaddafi and his wife were visiting the home when it was struck, but both were unharmed.

US Defense Secretary said that NATO was not targeting Gaddafi specifically, but his command and control facilities were legitimate targets. His military support commanded by his son, known as the Khamis Brigade, killed rebelling civilians. He also imported mercenaries from Nigeria, Belarus, Ukraine, and Serbia.

PRICE ON GADDAFI'S HEAD

AS FIGHTING GOES ON

Libya's new masters offered a MILLION dollar bounty for Gaddafi's HEAD, as fighting went on. Mummar Gaddafi strongly urged his men to fight on in battles across parts of the country. Gaddafi will not give up easily and could still unleash a "catastrophic event."

He urged Libya's tribes to "exterminate traitors, infidels and rats." Scattered pockets of loyalist diehards kept the irregular fighters at bay a day after rebel forces overran his Tripoli Headquarters, trashed symbols of his 41+ years rule and hunted Gaddafi and his sons. Rebels also reported fighting deep in the desert and there was a standoff round Gaddafi's tribal hometown.

Western leaders were readying, the hand over of Libya's substantial foreign assets, frozen from Gaddafi's assets overseas and were to be basically used against him. These will develop oil reserves that can make Libya (? & NATO COUNTRIES) richer.

"There are still many snipers in eastern Tripoli, "said one frontline fighter. "Finishing them will take lot of time."

Government buildings were being stripped of anything of value. At the Bab al-Aziziyah complex, fighters were still going through buildings that are hoarding sniper rifles and ammunition, which they distributed amongst their own ranks. Medical supplies were dwindling down to critical levels in several places. There were hundreds of casualties from the recent fighting needing emergency treatment, but these patients could not be saved due to lack of supplies. "The situation is out of control here," said a rebel spokesman. Appeals for normalcy were made in the streets, but shooting continued unabated. During gatherings in mosques appeals were made for blood DONATIONS, which had reached dangerously low levels in hospitals.

Gaddafi's tribal hometown of Sirte, on the coast between Tripoli and Benghazi was still not in the hands of the new leadership that have dispatched forces there.

Nor was the southern city of Sabha, where the rebels reported fighting.

Today is August 29, 2011 and I just picked up TIME magazine from my mail. There was an article headed *"ALL ROADS LEAD TO TRIPOLI"* on page 10 with a photograph of a gun-trotting rebel pointing towards the minaret of a mosque in the oil town of Brega. It is here that I spent over three years of my life working as an executive for Exxon Oil.

This picture reminded me of the very nice bungalows, we used to live in. The major conflict between President Reagan and Col. Gaddafi started around that time. American embassy was burnt and All-American workers and their families received the marching orders. President Reagan insisted on every one to come home to safety. My family was also evacuated and was very well looked after by the State Department. However I was asked to stay on. Top honchos of Exxon, on the topmost floors of the Exxon headquarters, at Avenues of America had other plans for me. Eventually I received a call from this top executive that they needed me to stay back in Brega.

The reality was that Gaddafi knew me as an Indian, not knowing my Immigration status and called me Professor because I reminded him of his actual Indian professor, during his student days.

He used to personally ask for me to set-up his, telephone, communications and electronic apparatus, whenever he landed up, unanounced! No one dare disclose his whereabouts.

The short briefs of the "TIME" stated that: The war in Libya appears to have lurched into a new, possibly a decisive phase. After weeks of slow grinding conflict, rebels fighting the forces of Muammar Gaddafi *were on the verge of making a push toward Tripoli, the capital. NATO air strikes had enabled rebel forces to take total control of the strategic town of Zawiyah, just west of the capital. In desperation, Gaddafi called for the residents of the city to take up arms in his defense. The rebels are confident that supporters and comrades inside Tripoli-where the regime's grip remained tightest-will rise*

65

up, once rebel fighters reach the capital. Elsewhere rebel fighters looked poised to capture the pivotal oil town of Brega. A scud missile fired at their advance by Gaddafi's forces landed miles off target, but despite significant gains doubts loom over the health of the rebel alliance: The July assassination of a prominent rebel commander exposed bitter tribal and political divides festering among the rebels

The above story reminds me of the following facts:

It relates to a topical situation and tends to convey observations depending upon their relationship with the conflicting sides involved in this story. A Gaddafi supporter will be convinced that these dumb rats should be burnt alive and his supporters did the heroic act of assassinating that evil commander. The rebel supporters and most of the readers in the western countries will be rejoicing to learn that the vicious dictator Gaddafi is about to fall. They demand that he be caught and hanged like Saddam Hussein, for his torturing the innocent poor. They will be saluting the efforts of the NATO forces and their gracious and humane support of the decent HAVE-NOTS who suffered for 41+ years at the hands of this greedy marauder and torturer. While the unconcerned majority who hate sensationalism would be disgusted at both sides. They will criticize the Western countries for meddling in other countries affairs and burning our hard earned $s, especially when every penny is needed to help our own homeless and unemployed 10%. They have the right to question the Government who can only exist with the taxes we pay, and are over buried in the debt and interest paid on them to countries like China whose large population has been taught to save from their childhood. The media moguls and the Hollywood films make their millions on sensationalism. For example the above news page is 70% covered by the photograph, which has nothing whatsoever to do with the news. An old photo obviously fits the architecture of the area. The soldier could be an actor posing for the shot, or they buy photos suited to the scene or activity!

Most of the news is not factual and the wording is carefully chosen. The heading is based on *ALL ROADS LEAD TO ROME*. The opening remarks using "appears to be" and "on the verge of making," is created to protect the editor from the law!

It is a well-known fact that NATO air strikes paid for by the American taxpayer is the only way Gaddafi's Airpowers could have been eliminated. This is how Gaddafi's rampage was halted.

Also every Lybian had been given a gun and plenty of ammunition these days, which was absolutely prohibited during Gaddafi's regime. His soldiers were forced to carry guns without bullets, which were meant to create enough fright. Now majorities of rag tag Libyan masses shout at the top of their lungs and keep on firing bullets in the air aimlessly, because it does not cost them a penny. These cost American taxpayers money that our government has to borrow, and for which 90% employed Americans, pay taxes as well. The other day these rebels who are learning warfare techniques as they go along, entered Gadaffi's private towers and spent hours leisurely discovering his underground winding tunnels and secret bunkers and helped themselves with his personal videos and paraphernalia.

Lots of cameramen and newscasters made hay! They found a book of pictures of smiling Condoleezza Rice, with lot of make up looking as if she is out to attract, in the personal bedroom of the Colonel? Some one shouted in Arabic, what he thought of what was going on there?

Revelry, Revenge, and loud shouts asking for "Catch and bring that Dictator to Justice" were repeated on the TV covering tons of bullets being wastefully fired in the air. Looked like a spoiled child using his first toy to impress his childhood girlfriend!

The reality is beautifully summed up in the last sentence-
"Tribal bitterness creates festering divide amongst the rebels."
And that my dear readers is a fact. Even in the days of the
"Lion of the Desert" a hand full of Sanussis under the
leadership of Umar al Mukhtar fought against huge war
machines and thousands of Italian soldiers landed from a
flotilla of war ships under direct orders from the Italian dictator
Benito Mussolini.

However one of Mukhtar's tribesman Idris1, also from
Cyranaica, used to hob knob with the British and lived the life
of a king.

This proves that no two tribes lived near each other nor stayed
in one area, and had no love lost between each other. The
fellows belonging to same tribes could be bitter enemies.
Simple example would be two 'Smiths' could belong to a
different heritage, different background, different convictions,
different attitude, standard of living, and mental make up!

Above all most of the war stories are observations not always
directly from the actual war sites, because no civilians should or
are allowed to be at the front line anyway. You see such scenes
in the movies. Here I remember the broadcast by the most
honored and award winning unbiased journalist Christiane
Amanpour during Iraq war. She said that the reporters who are
embedded with a particular battalion are never allowed within
miles of the point of skirmish, because of their safety and the
fighting position changes at high speed and numbers of clashes
differ on the spur of the moment.

WANING OF GADDAFI'S IMAGE

Gaddafi is already history in the eyes of the rebels and their
political leaders had already held high-level talks in Qatar on
Wednesday (24th Aug.), with envoys of United states, Britain,
France, Turkey and the United Arab Emirates on future

strategies. Next meeting was scheduled for Thursday, August 25th, 2011 in Istanbul.

The fall of Gaddafi, with the arresting images on Arab satellite TV of rebels stomping through his sanctum and laying waste to the props of his power, could invigorate other revolts in the Arab world, such as Syria where President Bashar al-Assad has launched bloody military crackdowns on protestors.

NATO warplanes bombed the compound as per al-Arabia TV, citing rebel sources. Rebels claimed they held three of Gaddafi's sons and one escaped. They also captured the powerful intelligence chief Abdullah al-Senussi. Commander Khamis had also been captured.

The rest of Libya is reeling with months of civil war, which has left tens of thousands dead. There are reports that on going NATO air strikes have landed wide of their mark, killing a number of civilians.

And some disturbing pictures of civil casualties in Libya are moving French lawyers to turn against their government.

French Ex-Foreign minister Roland Dumas says he is ready to defend Muammar Gaddafi in the international Criminal Court, which has issued a warrant for his arrest.

But NATO has to find the Colonel first, who is hiding for good reason. "If they find him they'll serve him to the sharks, Like they did to Bin laden, "Dumas said. "Some states are now claiming the right to kill, against all international law." *It is a jungle out there- and a shameful joke that nations MEDDLE in other countries affairs to establish Democracy there!*

Nicolos Sarkozy faces lawsuits over ordinary people killed in the war in Libya. Lawyers in France now accuse the president of committing crimes against humanity.

Jaques Verges calls the Libyan war a new Vietnam, where the US sprayed tens of thousands of liters of toxin on crops in the 60s and 70s causing brain disorders, miscarriages and birth defects to this day. "They are using missiles with depleted uranium, which cause cancer," he claimed. He added that "In Tripoli I saw people e.g. -office workers who had nothing to do with the fighting, but were crippled by NATO attacks. That is why we are suing President Sarkosy for crimes against humanity."

NATO first denied bombing the residence where 13 civilians, including four children, died. It then called the place a military command center. Journalist Michel Colon went to see what it really housed. " Books, videos, Spiderman toys, cultural books, nothing military," were what he saw there.
In another attack, Khaled El Awidi's wife, child and grandchildren were reportedly killed in their home; NATO is accused of deliberately waging a campaign of terror. "There bombings targeted the electricity, water and food supplies," Awidi's lawyer, Marcel Ceccaldi said. "After five months of daily NATO bombs and thousands of deaths, people will stop supporting the regime, because they cannot take it any more." Western leaders poised for their legal challenges have attempted to stop cases coming to courts. Ceccaldi adds that the politicians really run Western Justice.
Washington never took reports of Libyans representing Gaddafi, desperately wanting to negotiate with U.S., over last 2 days, seriously, because Gaddafi never indicated his willingness to step down.
French President Nicolas Sarkozy who took an early gamble on the rebels and may now reap political benefits, called on the Gaddafi loyalists "to turn their back on the criminal and cynical blindness of their leader by immediately ceasing fire." Later Sarkozy spoke to Britain's Prime Minister, David Cameron, and both agreed to pursue efforts in supporting the legitimate Libyan authorities as long as Gaddafi refused to surrender arms.

President Obama says that conflict is not yet over. He cautioned rebels against exacting revenge for Gaddafi's brutal rule. "True justice will not come from reprisals and violence," he said.

He made it clear that he will oppose any group within the loose coalition of rebels from imposing its power over other parts of Libyan society. Above all we call for an inclusive transition that leads to a democratic Libya."

Gaddafi's very close relations with Italy over a decade have taken a turn for the worse, because of his covert actions. Libya has long been a popular gathering point from where thousands of African immigrants have set sail to cross into Europe via Lampedusa off the southern coast of Sicily.

A deal between Gaddafi and Italy to send migrants back before they entered Italian waters curbed the flow of migrants—until the Libyan uprising earlier this year brought down strict border controls and drew a fresh wave of migrants.

Italy, once Gaddafi's biggest ally in Europe turned into a target of his rage after the former colonial power endorsed the Libyan rebel movement and joined a NATO campaign to oust the veteran leader.

Foreign Minister Franco Frattini said:

"We have terrible messages (in our possession) and they will be made public soon," Frattini said in an interview with Avvenire, the Italian bishop's newspaper. "We have proofs of orders given by Gaddafi's government to transform Lampedusa into an inferno: 'Put thousands of desperate people on boats and throw the island into chaos. 'We have proof and we cannot ignore it."

Italy has "messages" showing that Libyan authorities ordered civilian clothes to be put on the bodies of soldiers, so as to pin blame for their deaths on NATO, he said.

Since the uprising started, tens of thousands of migrants have arrived in Lampedusa, almost overwhelming the tiny island which was unprepared for the sudden deluge.

Chaos on the island turned into a massive headache for Prime Minister Silvio Berlusconi's conservative government, which came to power in 2008 and pledged to stop illegal immigration. The orders to put migrants on boats to Italy were given by Gaddafi himself, Libya's ambassador to Italy, Hafed Gaddur, who defected to the rebel side in February, told Italian radio. Hundreds of people have drowned attempting the dangerous crossing from North Africa to Lampedusa since the fighting started in Libya in February.

♠ ♣ ♥ ♦

MATTHEW VAN DYKE

He returned to his home in Baltimore on November 15, 2011, after serving as a rebel in Libya.

This is a clear case of foreigners who went in to support the rebels and directly oppose the mercenaries.

Van Dyke left for Libya in February, days after the uprising against Moammar Gaddafi began. He had made some friends there during his earlier travels to the Middle East and North Africa. He told his family that he is hoping to document that country's extraordinary events as a coda to a film and book he was working on. But apparently that was not his true intention. Sherry Van Dyke rallied local officials and the local media to keep her son's story alive.

In July a rumor surfaced that he was in Abu Salim.

Human rights official visited but could not find him.

Somehow by August, as rebels rounded up Gaddafi loyalists in Tripoli, his girlfriend in Baltimore got a call. It was Van Dyke. He had escaped from the prison after the guards had fled. He was dazed and had lost weight; the only clothing he had was his prison uniform.

However he had no intention of coming home while Gaddafi was at large. Instead he joined the fighting in Sirte. "I wasn't going to leave until Gaddafi was out of power," he said. " And now he's gone, so I am home."

Thin bearded and wearing rebel fatigue and a kaffiyeh on his head, he said, "I think I'm going to start training for the next Arab revolution that is spreading."

Eight months after he disappeared into the black hole of Libya's civil war, and in defiance of predictions that he disappeared in the desert, Matthew Van Dyke touched down Saturday night at the airport near his Baltimore home.

Some Commentaries on Gaddafi's Assassination

Below are some interesting comments, picked up from the international press, some are from Reuters and others from Twitter.

David Cameron hailed the death of the former Libyan strong man in October 2011. He was proud of the part played by Britain. This was a far cry from his insistence in March that Gaddafi be put on trial. Some suggest this was an execution and question why this is being applauded?

"Gaddafi was assassinated after he was caught wounded. This is a very heinous crime against a wounded man and the Arab public will see as such." Political analyst professor Ibrahim Alloush is convinced." I've talked to people who disliked Gaddafi and who disliked the way he was killed. They think this tells you something about the morality of the so-called revolutionaries." This view is shared on the Twitter. There are several posts already concerned about the coverage, questioning the necessity of such graphic images displayed, with jubilation. Another suggests the media outlets are having a competition. Sally Bercow, a prominent activist in the UK says she sees why the same was not done for Osama Bin Laden. Back then Obama did all this in great secrecy to avoid revenge from Al-Qaida. The images of Bin Laden's mangled body were not released for fear of inciting more violence.

But for Gaddafi the rag tag vultures were too quick and out of control. Also the untold numbers killed in the NATO intervention cast a dark shadow over their victory.

♠ ♣ ♥ ♦

REMEMBER LIBYA'S OIL & GAS RESOURCES ARE THE GREAT GEMS WORTH FIGHTING FOR!

(After oil production is restored, NATO, Allies will not bother about Libya, rebels, or NTC! That is the name of the game!)

In my humble opinion the following unique situations separates Libya from the rest of the Middle East, in the manner "Peace and Progress" may return here, and the time it will take to do so?

The bounty hunters would be Italy, France, and other European countries, which use and need Libyan type of Oil & Gas, and are close to it. The transportation costs are minimal. The economic situations in these European countries are deteriorating, with several of their currencies devaluing and their GDP falling. Some may eventually part company from Euro Currency?

China and India, has become more Oil dependent as time goes by.

The possibility of other Oil hungry countries with flourishing economies may join the fray.

NATO's ability and financial capacity to support the rebels, in the near and long-term future, may alter?

77

The interaction of the variant nomads from dozens of disunited tribes may attract outsiders who may create either more harmony or discord.

The worst situation could be evil mercenaries; Al Qaida, Russian Mafia, or even overflow of refugees from neighboring countries may join the Libyan revolution, because they have nothing to loose?

The swift military advance of recent days revived questions about the shadowy role of foreign Special Forces on the ground. First signs emerged of moves to begin restoring oil production that has been the foundation of the economy and a source of hope for Libya's six million, mostly poor people. Staff from Italy's ENI arrived to look into restarting facilities, said Franco Frattini. Italy is a big customer for Libya's energy. But it will face stiff competition from others seeking a share of Libya's wealth a competition some fear could test the ability of untried rebel leaders to hold the country together.

(Reporting by Peter Graff in western Libya)

The French President Nicolas Sarkozy was the first Western leader to bask in the gratitude of Gaddafi's opponents when he received rebel government chief Mahmoud Jibil in Paris. Sarkozy also took a lead in pushing for NATO military intervention. Sarkozy declared that Paris will host a "Friends of Libya" summit next Thursday, September 1, It would include **Russia and China**, both critics of Western bombing campaign which have been **concerned** at now **loosing out on business deals** with the rebels. France, Britain, and the United States were working on a new United Nations resolution to ease sanctions and asset freezes imposed on Libya when Gaddafi was in charge. Rebels also spoke of bringing back workers to restart oil export facilities soon. Fighters who swept into Tripoli at the weekend (September 3rd & 4th), uniting several fronts and a variety of opposition groups, were trying to establish order in the city, but faced pockets of resistance and several signs of looting. Snipers kept up fire from high buildings, including high points in the Gaddafi complex. Rebels blasted back with anti-aircraft guns mounted on pickup trucks. Imposing order and preventing breaking out of rivalries, across tribal, ethnic and ideological lines among the desperate rebel factions are major concerns of the new leaders and their Western backers, who are working to avoid the anarchy and bloodshed that followed after the overthrow of Iraq's Saddam Hussein. The rebels, many of whom were once Gaddafi supporters stressed the desire to work with former loyalists and officials, to avoid the purges of ousted ruling elite. The idea is to learn from Iraq's example where similar Purges caused Iraq's descent into sectarian anarchy after 2003. In Tripoli, even as a plethora of groups vie for inclusion in the new government, there are fewer and fewer checkpoints. There is little noticeable tension between the men with the guns and the general population. This is a far cry from the Iraq scene, with its chilling, ambush- prone roadblocks.

"I think if there were foreign troops here things would be much different," said Najwa Shalabi, who was taking her children to the park. "We trust the freedom fighters. They are Libyans all.
"We hope Iraq can be like us someday," said Shalabi before escorting her children towards the rickety-looking car.
Iraq has many times more tribes and clans, who are long time rivals, compared to thinly populated Libyans.
Also Libya is free from the Sunni vs. Shiias conflicts.

HOT REGIONAL NEWS

(Related to strife and turmoil. Protests, Financial crises,
& Natural Disasters, during Arab Spring 2011

EGYPT

NGOs say military is liquidating pro-democracy revolution to "take revenge" against Mubarak critics.

On the anniversary of Mubarak's removal from power unease reigns in Egypt.

Egypt forces raid pro democracy offices.

Military clashes with protesters-7 dead.

EGYPTIAN authorities agreed to halt raids against pro-democracy groups.

Egyptian court bans virginity tests? Protestors say they were threatened with prostitution charges before they were subjected to these tests.

Thousands protest in Tahrir Square: Thousands killed in confrontation and sectarian violence.

Lots of clashes took place between fans of opposing football teams!

Troops, Cairo protesters clash for second day.

LIBYA

Gaddafi's son under arrest in Niger.

Tripoli on high security alerts. Dozens of rebel vehicles patrolling streets in-groups.
Militia thwarts plot by Gadhaffi supporters to blow up Tripoli's power grid on New Year's eve.

Libya's NTC's say Moammer Gaddafi's killers will be brought to trial

Libya asks UN Security Council to hold up on lifting the no-fly zone!

NTC appoints Zintan's local military commander Osama Al-Juwali as defense minister.

Al Qaida trying to recruit in Libya.

USA seeks program to buy up loose missiles-the deadly legacy of the UPRISING in Libya.

NATO strikes killed and wounded dozens of civilians, but the alliance have largely refused to investigate unintended casualties.

UN Security Council returns over $40 million that will help new government to rebuild the country.

UN urges Libya to prevent revenge killings.

Gaddafi begged for Italy's help in letter.

Gaddafi's dead body was not open for public view and was buried at dawn in a secret location.

Bodies of Gaddafi loyalists were executed and dumped as garbage at Sirte Hotel!

Tripoli academic Abdul al-Raheem al-Qeeb was elected as Libya's interim Prime Minister.

NATO Chief Rasmussen declared that arms embargo is still in effect in Libya. He reiterated that NATO has no intention of building military basis there.
Libya's PM confirms presence of chemical weapons, says nation has no interest in keeping them.

LIBYA's Muslim Brotherhood meets freely in Benghazi after Gaddafi's demise.

UN Security Council votes to end Libyan operations on 31 Oct. 2011

Mass grave of 150 civilians executed by Gaddafi soldiers was found in Bin Javad. Innocent suffer the consequential damages- because is so unfair!

SYRIA
(Strangulating Siege in HOMS)

Fresh violence leaves 4 dead as Russia calls Arab League's initial assessment of country "reassuring"

(Conflicting reporting amongst power blocks)

Huge rallies have been met by lethal gunfire from security forces apparently worried about multiple mass sit-ins.

Defected Syrian Army killed 27 Syrian soldiers, stating that commanders had ordered killing peaceful protests "by all means necessary."

Hundreds of Thousands protest and demonstrate to the ARAB LEAGUE Monitors. Troops killed nine protestors in spite of Monitors presence!

International observers arrive in Syria amongst bloodshed. Bashar killed 23 more Syrians during violent crackdown.

Mass funeral for 44 killed in suicide bombings Mourners shout support for President Assad.

Growing ranks of former soldiers turn as rebels.

Death escalates as Syria mulls observers

TUNISIA

ARAB SPRING TURNS ONE YEAR OLD.

It was in Tunisia where it all started. *A desperate attempt by one Tunisian fueled the uprising all across the Arab world. A Tunisian fruit seller immolating himself in protest against corruption.*

Court decides to extradite former Libyan Prime Minister.

Tunisia and Egypt, its immediate neighbors to the west and east, Libya experienced a full-scale revolt beginning on 17 February 2011. By 20 February, the unrest had spread to Tripoli.

TUNISIA HONORS THE BIRTHPLACE OF ARAB SPRING

Festival in Sidi Bouzid remembers fruit vendor, protestors whose anger snowballed into region-wide phenomenon

SUDAN

President Bashir says his government gave arms, ammunition, and assistance to the Libyans.

YEMEN

More than 100,000 marching into Sanaa are met with guns water canons and tear gas-3 killed.

GADDAFI'S ASSASSINATION

(His burial in an undisclosed grave)

Mansour Dao one of his top security advisors told CNN that Gaddafi spent his final weeks, scavenging for food and hiding in abandoned houses in Sirte, bereft of the comforts and luxuries he was accustomed to. He had no electricity, TV but was engrossed in reading books he had brought in his suitcase. His behavior became "unpredictable" as the fighters advanced rapidly. He was worried and erratic when his plans to flee to his birthplace Jaref Village, 20 km, west of Sirte, did not materialize. According to the Hindu philosophy there is life after death. The soul leaves the body and enters in a new body just like you change your dress.
Obama's has developed a unique method of casting the bodies of his victims either to the sharks or to underground creatures to ensure no human can touch them. But when he has to report to the higher authority, the departed souls may track him down and come for

Revenge? Gaddafi almost adopted him as his son and wondered why he is out to kill him? Gaddafi's blood is being claimed by some to partially belong to Muslim brotherhood. *LIBYA IMPOSES VISA REQUIREMENTS ON EGYPTIANS AFTER EGYPT IMPOSED TRAVEL RESTRICTIONS!*
NATO's fuel truck was torched in Pakistan.
IRAN SOUNDS LIKE IRAQ 8 YEARS BACK.
Iraq was allegedly working on Libyan weapons, too: Former President George Bush's smoking gun," which also subsequently went missing. And on the basis of this 'intelligence" about Iraq's weapons of mass destruction" the United States and its more gullible allies invaded the country. Hundreds of thousands died, but no weapons of mass destruction were found. The war itself caused huge economic disaster that is still being felt by the 10% unemployed and the massive housing debacle.

A Rebellion started By a Dead Man

Even in death Muammar Gaddafi casts a long shadow. During the peak of his regime he spent hundreds of hours sowing seeds of discord, arming insurgents and plotting coups in other parts of Africa.

That habit continues after his brutal assassination and shameless treatment by the rebels aided by the airpowers of NATO allies. Wielding weaponry from Gaddafi's arsenal, ethnic Tuareg rebels clashed with Malian armed forces and launched ruthless blatant attacks on several towns.

The Tuareg, a Saharan tribe who has been struggling for greater autonomy for ages were the elite Gaddafi mercenaries. As his hold on power slipped, due to western intervention, many returned home and brought their anti-tank weapons with them. Now the armed uprising in Libya that ousted Gadhafi from power albeit with NATO air supports — appears to have breathed new life into the Syrian revolt. "Our souls, our blood we sacrifice for you; Libya!" Syrian protesters chanted Friday. Others held signs linking Assad's fate to those of other deposed Arab leaders. Tunisia's Zine El Abidine Ben Ali has been driven into exile. Egypt's Hosni Mubarak is in jail. He is facing charges of complicity, in the deaths of more than 800 protesters, during the uprising.

Gadhafi is killed, but Assad is in *FULL CONTROL*."

Gadhafi's death Thursday, after he was dragged from hiding in a drainage pipe, begging for his life, decisively ended the nearly 42-year regime that had turned the oil-rich country into an international pariah and his own personal fiefdom.

In many ways, the Syrian uprising has taken cues from the Libyans recently. Internal divisions during its tenure as Libya's interim governing authority have plagued the National Transitional Council. It postponed the formation of a caretaker, or interim government on several occasions during the period prior to the death of Muammar Gaddafi in his hometown of Sirte on 20 October 2011.

LIBYA'S TRYST WITH DESTINY

Since the overthrow of Muammar Gaddafi's government, there has revived hopes that an open society will encourage the return of tourists.

Prior to the uprising, Saif al-Islam Gaddafi, the second-eldest son of Muammar Gaddafi, was involved in a green development project called –The Green Mountain's Sustainable Development Area. He sought to bring tourism to Cyrene and to preserve Greek ruins in the neighborhood. But that concept was killed when Saif was locked up by the rebels who called him 'KINKY HEAD."

As per the views of Aijaz Zaka Syed on Libya's Tryst with Destiny dethroning Gaddafi was the easy part; the real struggle begins now.

We are living in truly interesting times as the Chinese would say.

Whosoever we are and where ever we are we shall cherish the 2011-year as remarkable for the Middle East. It is not every day that the mighty men who have forced their will over and controlled the destiny of millions of people for several decades, come crashing down and were buried in secret grounds or fed to the predators in the deep blue ocean mercilessly.

The Libyan people have finally joined the Egyptians and Tunisians in celebrations and are rejoicing the disappearance of their tormentor after forty-two years of vile, total tyranny. This is not just the zonal victory but the epic triumph for us all who believe in freedom, human dignity, and individuals that believe in the people's right to choose their destiny. This is the best Ramadan Libyans have had in decades. And this EID the Libyans will have their celebrations doubled. Indeed this will be a special Eid for the Egyptians and Tunisians as well.

Freedom from tyranny, Freedom from fear and Freedom from indignity are the greatest gifts of all.

The handicap faced by the NTC will be the vacuum of institutional infrastructure left by Gaddafi. There was just a single man Government, tyranny and abuse of Power to suit his personal ownership of the country, its people and its oil and other resources.

The NTC have a daunting task ahead of them and probably no time to celebrate. People who have managed to surmount the greatest and daring challenges to their very existence with determination and enduring faith can transcend any obstacles.

Across the pond the western nations are over jubilating and backslapping for their support to the Libyan people.

Of course the NATO bombing targeting Gaddafi forces- and many innocent civilians- has played a significant part in tilting the scales against the tyrant.

However the steadfastness, initiative and monumental sacrifices of the Libyan people brought this dawn of hope and progressed to the bitter reality.

It was the infectious courage and resolve of ordinary Libyans that forced the Arab and Muslim nations to give up their cautious indifference.

Gaddafi's fate, and like that of his other disgraced peers, should be a wake-up call to others who have all these years abused the sacred trust and the responsibility thrust upon them. The ignominious end of Gaddafi will surely hasten the departure of the Salehs and Assads of the world. The longer they drag the final day, the greater humiliation will be their fate.

"We shall see when the Insurmountable mountains of oppression blow as if cotton flakes. The land will throb with a deafening sound."
Faiz Ahmed Faiz

Having looked at the big picture of the universe and our own GLOBE, we are back to facing the real challenge of guessing the real future of Libya.

Our observations will be judged by the real happenings in the future so we must arrive at the best judgements based on analyzing the present.

At this stage I remember my visit to a local circus where they showed how the trainer of three tigers, controlled them from pouncing on him simultaneously. His brain was super-alert and he kept a constant and consistent super speed watch on all of them and used the communication skill of his eyes staring at theirs. In reality this is a metaphor of the actual trainer being "Libya's Destiny,"

While the three tigers are represented by the following:

The disunited Nomads who live in far fetched parts of the vast desert, each agreeing to disagree with other groups!

The *WIDENING GAP* between those who *HAVE*, and uneducated, easy to be swayed *HAVE-NOTS*. Foreign influences, mercenaries, and political diverse groups are consistently tempting them to fight with them to promote their selfish cause. There is an abundance of weapons, and Weapons of Mass Destruction "out for grabs."

The ARAB Spring Movement and *THE PENDULUM SWINGS*, is the metaphor for the ever-changing Politics of Convenience with basic two parties coming in and going out of Power in the United Kingdom as well as between Democrats and Republicans in USA forever changing foreign policies. The *PENDULUM SWINGS HOURLY, IN EUROPE*, in these days of economic distress.

The western and *NATO* group, including *FRANCE, ITALY AND GERMANY* who are eagerly awaiting to dip in to the OIL WEALTH, now that they have successfully eliminated the only guy who kept them away from it.

THE FIRST ANNIVERSARY OF ARAB SPRING

THE DEGRADABLE DEPRAVITY OF THE DERELICTS

HAVES!

AGAINST THE POWERLESS HELPLESS UNEMPLOYED

HAVE-NOTS!

(Final, Fierce and pitched battles unto death between the invincible masses of *HAVE-NOTS*, and the Indomitable Billionaire Gaddafi.)

HAVE-NOTS REVOLTED AGAINST "HAVES." in Egypt, Tunisia, Yemen, Bahrain, Syria, Jordan, and Saudi Arabia and believe it or not in Israel as well!

POOR SUFFER BIG TIMES, MOST OF THE TIME.

THE INNOCENT GETS CAUGHT IN CROSSFIRE BETWEEN THE WARRING NATIONS.

FACT THAT MANY NATO AIR STRIKES LANDED WIDE OF THEIR MARK, RESULTING IN $80 MILLION WORTH OF TOMAHAWK MISSILES GOING INTO SMOKE, KILLING INNOCENT BYSTANDERS AS AN UNINTENDED CONSEQUENCE HAS BEEN MENTIONED IN WIDESPREAD NEWS COVERAGES!

In avoiding American interference Obama was following the principal of once bitten twice shy. He had been shouting from the election campaigning platforms that Bush's Iraq war was a mistake, we paid dearly for!

President Obama insisted on a genuine request for international help, from a local united front that was dedicated and willing to wage war against a ruthless dictator. He did not want USA help to be misconstrued as Western Imperialism in Muslim lands, even though certain Arab countries were drawn into the coalition. He insured that American help was financial and Air Strikes were routed through NATO. The lessons of Iraq are clear, in that Bush decided to prevail in Iraq at any cost, even if it meant massive increase in forces to quell what had turned out to be a raging civil war between religious factions. It was lucky that he was replaced before he could do more damage. The Shiias/Sunnis clashes could have turned ugly and a world war could have flared up involving all Muslim nations! The Prime Minister and other Bush appointees were not popular public figures. Therefore now that Obama is withdrawing American soldiers, another chaos and/or civil war could ensue?

The Libyan war cost of 0.1 percentage of the Iraq war cost of $1 trillion. 5,000 Americans and 10,000 Iraqi deaths can be compared with zero American and minimal Libyan casualties.

Donald Rumsfeld, then Defense Secretary when asked about chaos, looting and reprisal, killings, and unacceptable mistreatment of prisoners of war, shrugged his shoulders and quipped "Stuff happens," Compared to the present Robert Gates warning the president that enforcing "*NO FLY ZONE,*"

96

in Libya is an act of war. Just like prohibiting a country, from the use of their sovereign airspace!

The interference by West in Libya could be redesigned to offer a new model of humanitarian mission with strategic interest if there is a genuine desire and willingness to share the burden of the legitimate populace. I am sure it will stay as my dream unless Libyans can produce a miracle.

On the other hand the NTC have to bite the bullet and avoid taking revenge against the gigantic pain and cruelty caused by Gaddafi in the recent past. It is understandable that any victory against oppression leads to punishing the tyrant to teach him a lesson but I would recommend:

Do not lower yourselves to his level

Punishing him will include punishing his old guard, many of whom have joined the new *NTC*.

It will set a good name and good start if *NTC* does not copy the rotten style of the old regime but lifts its head high and gets recognized by the common Libyan and the world at large as such.

The question is what caused the revolts by the Have-nots to topple their Billionaire tyrants, other than unemployment, ability to team up undetected under the modern advanced social media, the youth and under utilization?

The Have-nots in Cairo and Tunis were ARAB and had a fast and peaceful assembly to bring down their dictators. Both happened during spring of 2011

But neither had any effect on the despots in Manama and Sanáa! Why? Bahrain is religiously divergent for centuries and may not have coherent youth forces.

Also in Bahrain and Yemen there was no Army that is against the tyrant, and pro- masses as in Egypt!

NATO has been providing the *AIR COVER* and flooding their arsenal with arms and ammunition.

That little push strengthens the rebel's unity.

The Logistics and financial help originate from USA.

Most of the top hierarchy of *NTC* is in close touch with the Obama administration in an orderly fashion. *NTC* consists of former respected Justices, scientists and peaceful revolutionaries who recently resigned from Gaddafi's receding regime. The biggest disaster in the *NTC* setup was when Gaddafi assassinated their top general on July 28.

Gaddafi's violent response had the opposite effect. It prompted defections of good people from his government. Gaddafi's "number 2" key man, Abdul Fatah Younis, as well as Mustafa Abdel-Jalil and several key ambassadors and diplomats resigned from their posts in protest. Some others were jailed for disobedience, as they refused to follow his orders.

As Gaddafi returned from his hideout in early March, relying on considerable amounts of Libyan & US cash, hidden in the capital, his forces progressed and retook all lost grounds within shooting range of Benghazi. This initiated the *NATO 'NO FLY ZONE.'* Support and Gaddafi soon lost his superior edge, his AIR POWER.

Gaddafi and his wife escaped while his son was hit a day after Gaddafi appeared on the state TV calling for talks with NATO to end the air strikes which have been hitting Tripoli. He suggested that there was room for negotiations. US Secretary of Defense Robert Gates confirmed that the UN Security Council resolution that authorized air campaign did not allow hitting Gaddafi and his family. But behind the scene he was trying to drive a wedge between Gaadfi's faithful top ranking commanders, and support suspect mercenaries?

As predicted in earlier pages Tripoli was attacked fiercely and almost fell in the hands of the protesters who went wild probing and turning his Tripoli compound upside down, and inside out. Tripoli could be taken over by the rebels, after complete eviction of the tyrant.

UN referred the massacres of unarmed civilians to the International Criminal Court. One of the crimes under investigation is the purchase and authorizing the use of Viagra like drugs amongst soldiers for the purpose of raping women and instilling fear.

Killing civilians indiscriminately is a charge of crimes against humanity under Article 7 of the Rome Statute of Criminal court.

There is a great potential of the hazardous TRIBAL WAR in Libya now that the strong man Gaddafi has been eliminated unceremoniously!

* * * * * *

Watching and listening are a great art
By watching and listening we learn
Infinitely more than we do from any books.
Books are necessary, but watching
And listening sharpens your senses

LIBYAN REBELS FIGHT EACH OTHER FOR POWER

As per a recorded phone call on September 19, 2011

There is a dispute between Misurata rebel leader and Col. Ahmed Bani, a spokesman for *NTC*, showing several rebels' lies and hypocrisies. They talk about the presence of U.S. and French troops within Misurata, and Tripoli. They clearly admit that they are still there.

Misurata commander was critical of the *NTC*'s gloating about the so-called New National Army, while Gaddafi laid Misery over Misrata and crushed the National army at Dafniya, till a few bragging top brass were parading on TV. He challenged them to come to Benghazi and fight in the actual battlefield! He told them to stop acting like the Americans and French, like Sarkozy parading while war is still going on.

He complained that they never got the weapons promised to them nor seen any troops or mercenaries from Qatar, after 150 millions were spent on this deal.

He swore that those in Benghazi who betrayed them would pay a heavy price, after this revolution. This is yet another of many hurdles plaguing, the future progress of the country.

Wounded by *NATO*'s drone attack, Gaddafi ran for shelter to the nearest concrete drainpipes at the local construction site. He was bleeding, and became unconscious.

Libyan newspaper the "JAMAHIRIYA WARIOR" dated October 15, 2011 published the following @ 10:15AM (5 days before he was killed.)

Sirte

Urgent calls to the Global Community-

The religious leaders of Sirte (Libya) have issued a FATWA authorizing the surviving residents to eat dogs and cats. About one month ago some 3000 soldiers and 80000 civilians were trapped in the city, besieged by the forces of the *NTC* overseen by the officers of *I. C. C.* (International Criminal Court,) and bombed by *NATO*.

Sirte no longer received food supplies. Electricity and Water were cut off. Hospitals had stopped functioning.

The city was in ruins. Only 10000-20000 people managed to get away during the lulls in bombing and escaped sudden death.

No one believes *NATO*'s claim that its intervention in Libya served to protect the civilian population and that it will continue its work until the surrender or death of Muammar Gaddafi.

However *NATO*'s siege and bombardments constitutes war crimes according to the standards and principals of international law, considering that the main victims were the civilian population.

This is an undisputed fact and happens during each and every conflict, War, or world Wars. Innocent bystanders, public, unarmed children and women who are least prepared, or involved are the worst hit!

The Media and political leaders of the *NATO* zone, including the French who are too engrossed in their presidential election campaigning are ignoring this drama. A SILENCE which makes them all accomplices.

Secretary General of the Arab League A. Moussa said, "What is happening in Libya, differs from the aim of imposing a NO-FLY zone." He specifically condemned report of civilian casualties. Russia, India and China abstained from UN Security Council votes and condemned air strikes causing civilian death.

# # # #

<u>NATO</u> turned out to be the worst criminal
(putting Gaddafi to shame.)

UN Security Resolution 1973 authorizes the use of "all necessary measures…to protect civilians and civilian populated areas." "It further establishes ban on <u>all</u> flights in the airspace of the Libyan Arab Jamahiriya in order to protect civilians." Nowhere does it authorize US or NATO to provide military support to Libya's armed rebels fighting to overthrow Muammar Gaddafi.

Liberal Democrats-the heart and soul of Obama's meteoric rise to the White House, and Republicans are condemning administration's decision to send US forces to help Libyan rebels to ruthlessly oust the Libyan leader. They are also charging Obama with hypocrisy.

Simply put heavy bombing like Tomahawks does destroy a much wider area, and thousands of unintended casualties ensue. In ground fight where the direct targets are close at hand, innocents seldom get caught in cross fires. Even the press people stay away from harm's way

Poor and innocent suffer all the time, every time. Americans killed million unsuspecting Japanese when they threw Atom Bomb in Hiroshima and Nagasaki etc. The experts could not have predicted the quantum of damage and the Human, and Property loss suffered, by those who were neither an enemy nor caused harm to American forces. They were simple unsuspecting civilians who were massacred in that genocide, and carnage. It was huge, and altogether unnecessary.

Even the forward bombing squads involved felt so guilty that they suffered psychological damage!
I personally knew Leonard Cheshire, the British Airforce Bomb Squad leader who bombarded Berlin during world war and won all the top medals. He was so mentally disturbed and felt guilt from God that he devoted the rest of his life building "Cheshire Homes" for the terminally, helplessly hopelessly ill patients to take care of them during their last days on earth.
He had set up some homes in USA, but I worked with him as a social worker in setting up CHESHIRE Homes for the Leprosy patients, in the remote corners of India.

The blatant instability prevails in the streets of Tripoli today, four months after the shameful treatment given to Gaddafi by the uncontrolled hooligans, belonging to the rival militias backed by the NATO pack.
The sparring militias from the cities of Zintan and Misratah-brigades who were supported by the interfering NATO foreigners from the air after Gaddafi was forced out of his own sovereign airspace, are now vying for control of strategic locations, like Tripoli Airport.
These incidents are the glaring examples of the unmanaged chaos, in the country riven by Tribal and Regional splits and flush with guns.

The February 16, 2012 edition of the TIME magazine had the following news:

Fighters still loyal to Gaddafi briefly captured the town of Bani Walid- This convinced me that October killing of Gaddafi and the catastrophic killing of thousands of civilians, including genocide in Sirte would not have been possible without willful *NATO* intervention and support.

NATO's secret report based on interviews with some 4000 captured Taliban fighters claims that elements within Pakistan's military and government were still backing the Islamist insurgency in Afghanistan.

Times of London proclaim that the conviction in Kabul and Washington deepens. Pakistan's foreign minister obviously dismisses the whole report, but as trust between USA and Pakistan slumps, she may need to be more convincing.

Let us hope Libya's new leaders will learn from History and do not end up turning on their own people and abuse power.

Lets not forget Gaddafi, Iraq's Saddam Hussein, Tunisia's Ben Ali, and Syria's Hafez Assad, whose son is now trying to outdo him in cruelty, and many others had all thrown up previous regimes, promising the moon to their people and look where and how they ended up? Road to hell is paved with good intentions.
But the Libyans and for that matter the Tunisians, the Egyptians and others are capable of dealing with all those vultures waiting in the wings-waiting to move in for the big kill. Western powers do themselves no justice if they believe they can arm-twist Gaddafi's
Inexperienced successors into signing on the dotted line. The people of Libya are watching.

They are in no mood for more clever colonial games. The West must not squander the goodwill it has earned itself with such shenanigans.

Let us take the Americans and their *NATO* allies on their empty words that their support for freedom is not underpinned by the thirst for oil and all the riches waiting to be explored and exploited in Libya. Then USA and their comrades–in-arms across the pond should be able to support the cause of the Palestinians and Syrians as well. Let Washington, London and Paris spread the cheer all around and bless the Palestinians demand for statehood when it comes up at the United Nations next month.

While the Libyans have struggled for freedom for past six months, the Palestinians have pined for it for the past six decades. They have been breaking their heads against the Israel. Israel got rid of Palestinian freedom fighter and occupied their land and kept all anti USA elements at bay. They are acting like the Little America that has been fielding as Quarter backs in the Middle East. They are virtually the forward ranks of the USA's army in disguise for emergency actions. It reminds me of the British India Army where Gurkhas were always the first to face enemy bullets in wars.

Furthermore, how will the immensely diverse culture of the Libyan people and the many leaders of the revolution (all armed to the gunnels) now react to this new freedom, and who will actually govern them? How will they reach a collective agreement in this crucial aim and objective?

For as Franz Kafka said "Every revolution evaporates and leaves behind the slime of a new bureaucracy." Moreover, as Albert Camus opined, "all modern revolutions have ended in the reinforcement of the power of the state"-whoever or whatever the composition of the state may eventually comprise. Every one knows that without *NATO PROTECTION* the *NTC* cannot rule Libya for a single day. This is simply because what has happened in Libya was not a spontaneous revolution (by all the people of all walks of life) as was the case in Tunis and Egypt. It was a 'turn-key revolution' designed in France/UK/USA and was executed on the ground by some turncoats and carpetbaggers. This turnkey-project-revolution included banners, protesters, media coverage; some clowns to appear in front of cameras or interviewed in talk-shows etc.) The crucial item missing in this turnkey revolution was the supply of who will rule Libya next? Sarkozy, Cameron, Berluconi (or his replacement), Obama? What about sending Dr. Gonzi to rule Libya?

Before getting into the Afghanistan scenarios we may stop over for few moments on the Iraq war. On May 1, 2003 President Bush announced Major Combat Operations in Iraq Have Ended. Actually the war had just begun after this date. Will same thing happen in Libya?

Libyan people are now declaring themselves to be "Free" and those who died fighting on the barricades at the gates of Heaven, as martyrs.

What was the price for this perceived Liberty?

Sadly, the dead heroes were seen as dispensable pawns in the great and convoluted game of chess played by *NATO* members to achieve their avaricious and perfidious aims and objectives; The eventual obscene land, power or resource grabbed shall lead to the squabbles that will inevitably follow.

These games of Heaven, now breached by the freedom fighters, may regrettably turn out to be the entrance to another domain, belonging to Hades.

May their God guide and protect the Libyan people, as they will now need all the help they can get! (*Times of Malta, Saturday, October 29, 2011, by Peter Murray, Mosta*)

Robert Bridge, RT.- reports that after the disappearance of Gaddafi average Libyans face daily challenges to survival with the lack of food, water, and fuel. He predicts that after oil pumping normalizes and NATO leaves, Libya will become a "puppet" state under the sway of international companies.

THE NATIONAL TRANSITIONAL COUNCIL

(IN LIBYA)

USA says, that they are acting carefully in Libya, learning from mistakes in handling the situation in Iraq. As a result, the Libyan operation has been remarkably cost-effective. The National Transitional Council, is being designed with the following criteria in mind:

Plan to occupy and stabilize the country once the regime collapses, to avoid the reoccurrence of chaos, looting, and reprisal as it happened in Iraq. The Libyan opposition has been working diligently to avoid a recurrence of such mistakes.

In Iraq the Coalition Provisional Authority had disbanded the military and began a de-Baathification plan, purging administrators of all kinds-including local situation experts and teachers. It had also shutdown most of Iraq's state owned companies, because they were seen as socialist enterprises out of line with the "NEW IRAQ," viz. a "free–market paradise with flat tax. What actually happened was that these moves dislodged and removed the power from long standing ruling elite, who felt unwelcome in the new set up? They in turn were forced to launch a resistance to the new order.

The *NTC* consists of senior level respected and peace loving people like Mahmoud Jibril, who are earnestly planning far ahead and are really aware of the fact that the world is watching them. Jibril had put out a statement, urging the rebels not to loot, engage in reprisals, or in any way "sully the final page of the revolution." when Tripoli began to fall into their hands.

In Benghazi the council feels, it would be worth the effort to tame down the passions of revenge and anger against the 42 years reign of madness and cruelty, causing unforgettable pain and turmoil.

They themselves have defected from the regime and want to try to make the transition as inclusive as possible, without excommunicating the old guard and creating another division, or parting of ways. Luckily there is no religious divide and hatred as was the case with Sunnis in Iraq and Pashtun in Afghanistan!

In situations like these you can usually have justice or you can have order, but you cannot have both.

The Libyan intervention offers a new model for the West -a humanitarian mission together with strategic interests. Providing both the supports for ARAB SPRING, and new aspirations for the next generation. Avoiding the pitfalls of Iraq war is daunting enough, but it is the one they have eagerly sought and one for which they will find readily available help from friends around the world.

The main thrust of the *NTC* is to try to allay fears of bloody revenge taking, by the rebels. Their slogan shll be:

"WE WILL BUILD A NEW LIBYA, WITH ALL LIBYANS AS BROTHERS."

We do not see any circumstances in which Western powers would deploy troops on the ground in Libya.

Both President Obama and the British Prime Minister have declared that they will not risk loosing their military personnel on the ground war, in Libya. But some governments have had civilian advisors in Benghazi for months.

There are concerns of future harmony between newly liberated neighbors. Tribal wars could breakout between supporters of the clan, Gaddafi belonged to, and those who oppose his tribe. Also within the same tribe there had been opposing forces 180 degrees apart. For example the Lion of the desert and the King Idris were both Sannusis, two extremely opposite personalities. One being a "fighter unto death, father of the nation" and other a puppet of the British rulers. In 2011, exactly 100 years later, Gadhafi's close relative, another commander Sanussi, also a specialist negotiator landed up in USA, to make a deal with the Americans, on Gadhafi's behalf while fight to overthrow Gaddafi was stalemating. Rebel leadership lacked public appeal.

This country led by a fierce ruthless "Dictator sans merci," with an iron fist leaves behind weak and unreliable institutions, that do not possess self starting type initiative and wherewithal.

The minute Gaddafi is killed or captured, various groups will vie for the ownership of the revolution! It is not certain that the *NTC* could preside over the transitional vacuum? Struggle for power usually leads to blood shedding! However rebels have earned the benefit of the doubt by showing very little propensity for vendetta when they took charge of one town after another en route to Tripoli! But perhaps the credit goes to the foreign advisors and experienced employees of the Western group of nations, who supplied money, military equipment and logistic and technical know how?

NTC managed to maintain law and order in the rebel stronghold of Benghazi region, despite the assassination of their top general on July 28. They remained united and focused. One view was that they had to do that as they were under attack from Gaddafi's forces. Also leaders like Gebril a political scientist respected throughout the Middle East guided them.

Libyans (not foreigners,) marching into Tripoli gave this revolution an unquestionable legitimacy.

This legitimacy was further reinforced by the actions the *NTC* chairman Mustafa Abdel Jalil, a former Justice Minister took in impressing Obama Government to recognize *NTC* as Libya's unofficial government and authorizing a group of diplomats to Benghazi, to seal the deal.

The ingredients needed for the birth of a revolution is:

Large groups of tortured masses facing a common enemy, usually a heartless, arrogant and corrupt tyrant.
A huge unemployment occasion, and a group of lawyers and Judges of the Libyan High courts protesting in front of the

111

central jail, for the release of innocent political prisoners, being tortured!

Soaring food prices and rampant corruption.

Mass propaganda and political news.

Col. Gaddafi pledged "martyrdom or victory," in the fight against *NATO* (who destroyed his personal compound by 64 air strikes already), and the rebels.

Borrowing a page from the Libyan rebels, Syria's opposition groups announced the following day that they were setting up a national council.

It's better to give their revolution a recognizable identity.

" We don't think that military action is the way to go with Syria," says a senior Obama Administration official. For one thing Assad's military has greater firepower than Gaddafi's was. For another, the Arab League has not called for foreign interference in Syria.

But if you ask me the real reason could be that there is no Oil wealth to go after!

Today September 10, 2011, Gaddafi loyalist and rebels had a bitter fight over the occupation of a town called Beni Walid. But heavy *NATO* Air Bombing (costing American and other taxpayers several millions of dollars) easily settled the issue.

Thus Western Powers with their military might and most powerful Air Power, in the world, are in control and can decide whom they want to be the ruler in any country. The first target in the Arab Spring Tunisia's Ben Ali, was quickly followed by its second, bigger prize, Egypt's Mubarak.

Syrians hope Gaddaf's removal will hasten Bashar Asssad's, departure.

Even as Tripoli fell, the Syrian President pronounced, in an interview, with a reporter on state TV, "I am not worried."

During our brief encounter 29+ years ago, till this day I have never understood what Gaddafi really wanted to achieve in his Green Book? He forced it on me, to read and understand it or perhaps just wanted to hear me praise its depth, but I sincerely failed to find anything praiseworthy. He never had the capacity to judge the cause and effects when he acted furiously and on the spur of the moment. People in his capacity and circumstance cannot think deep and judge others around them, because they are drunk with an overdose of their own ego, and become "I" specialists. He was psychologically self centered and deeply believed that he was a very popular leader, dearly and honestly loved by the Libyan masses. Actually that was farthest from the truth. He lost most of his physical energy in marketing himself. His attacks on the west were verbal.

He demonstrated his anger by pumping fists in the air in synch with the slogans by his loyal followers. He never really had trained his small army in modern warfare and his Air Force was no match to Israelis, leave alone the western powers. He would not even allow bullets to be carried by his volunteer forces consisting of young students, mostly girls.

When the masses took to the streets, shouting for his resignation he used his petty means of repression, and crushed the revolt by hiring thugs from his son's Khamis brigade. He always underestimated **the Strength in unity** amongst peaceful demonstrators. He lost a golden opportunity of suppressing the outcry of the poor by peaceful negotiations and ignored Obama's request to calm the opposition or just step down.

It is not within their heart and mind to judge the reality of the situation, because their brain works in narrow channels seeking revenge. This encouraged all the western alliances to channel their attack through *NATO* and rebels who were begging their help and support.

Once Gaddafi was pushed against the walls and was contained, all he could do was fly into oblivion. That resulted in the whole world opinion, building up against him. He lost all chances of negotiations as an equal and opposite party coming to mutually acceptable terms. Now he had nothing!

Prime Minister David Cameron said the death of the former dictator is a day to remember all of Col. Gaddafi's victims. He was responsible for those who died in connection with the Pan Am flight over Lockerbie. Yvonne Fletcher in a London street, and obviously the victims of IRA terrorism who died through the use of Libyan Semtex.

The new national flag was raised above large utilities building in the Mediterranean City, which had been under siege for two months.

The post Gaddafi road ahead for Libya is fraught by any estimate.

Tens of thousands (several of them innocent by-standers in the

crossfire) might have died in the civil war. Actual numbers could take years to verify.

Already the wounded and maimed (both civilians and fighting rebels) are attacking the *NTC* for its failure to bring them speedy relief.

The biggest threat to peace in Libya is from the power struggle amongst the victorious factions.

The *NTC* leaders first raised the banner of revolt in Benghazi in February 2011. The Misrata militia who did much of the fighting, lost the most people and see themselves as the "Spartans" of the new Libya, and the fighters from the Nafusa mountains who tipped the balance against Gaddafi in august. In reality none of them did any thing great because *NATO* did the real damage to Gaddafi's rag tag army by their superior air power, but none of that will enter into the impending clashes between the above factions.

I PREDICT LOTS OF LITTLE GADDAFI'S CROPPING UP TO SHOW OFF THEIR IMPLIED CONTRIBUTIONS. THE WILD, FREE FOR ALL FIGHTS WILL HOLD UP THE FUTURE PROGRESS.

The legacy of repression and abuse from Gaddafi's rule will not end until there is a full accounting for the past and human rights are embedded in Libya's new institutions. Remember the *NTC* and the independent rebels in the FREE-FOR-All rag tag armies and all others who chipped in this war had done enormously more severe violations of human rights, compared to Gaddafi and on him.

Many Libyan officials suspected of serious human rights *VIOLATIONS COMMITTED DURING AND BEFORE THIS YEAR'S UPRISING, INCLUDING THE INFAMOUS* Abu Salim prison massacre in 1996, must answer for their crimes.

Amnesty international called on the *NTC* to ensure that all those suspected of human rights abuses and war crimes, including Gaddafi's inner circle and family members, are treated humanely and if captured, given fair trials. Amid widespread disbelief at the NTC claim that Gaddafi was caught in crossfire, and extreme hatred for them as puppets of the USA and western powers who blatantly interfered into Libya in spite of the friendly relationship between USA/UK/and Gaddafi.

This is a sad day for the people of Africa.

It is a far cry from the days of Gaddafi regime of 42 years wherein he became a strident anti-colonialist.

However his disastrous attitude in keeping the metric system out and enforcing his *"GREEN BOOK" ON PEOPLE*, will be thrown out of the window. His whole attitude of keeping millions of youth illiterate, and lacking in the knowledge about the modern advancement in I-Phone/I-Pads and other media of independent communications, was purely selfish and over possessive.

Ministry of Education's eyes is set on more immediate goals such as:

Getting rid of compulsory subject like Al-Mujtama Al-Jamahariya, the study of the GREEN BOOK –Gaddafi's core treatise on politics and civic life. Changing all symbols in Libyan education to meet the International standards. They have already changed several Arabic symbols into Latin script and corrected many spelling errors.

History, which was designed to glorify Gaddafi personally and his regime is being re-written from scratch. This subject has been suspended from national curriculum until the new books have been published. The temporary curriculum and textbooks are set to roll out and available to a million Libyan students. Until then the classes continue at places like the Rixos Technical High School in Tripoli.

The larger goal of removing the false ideas and mentalities cultivated through the 42 years of indoctrination may take quite a long time.

The big challenge remains the little kids who love Gaddafi and do not know why they love him.

17 years-old Epthal Abu Bakker said that whenever she used to criticize Gaddafi, other kids would tease her and beat her. Now things have changed and she is free to express her views openly.

" We have to know, the children have to know, what they missed before, "Epthal said. "About the grandparents, the old peoples, how they were. We have to find out why Gaddafi came, and why he did all that."

With the dictator gone Libya's future is ever more uncertain-the country is awash with weapons, and the revolutionaries are finding it hard to reconcile their differences and be good citizens.

The horizon is relatively bright-but this cannot continue unless the country's political journey continues smoothly.

'What next' is always an interesting question?

A country should always determine their own future or should they?

America has a vested interest in what happens in Libya.

We put our citizens in harms way to overthrow Gaddafi, so we should ensure their lives were not put in jeopardy to help replace one despot with another? If they ever want to ask me I would tell them that they should have never gone to Libya in the first place!

The next question everyone is asking is 'what Next?' followed by 'What now?'

Leaked UN *report reveals torture, lynching and abuse in post-Gaddafi* *Libya is rampant.*

Rebel militias in Libya are illegally detaining thousands of people, including women and children. Many of the prisoners are suffering torture and systematic mistreatment while being held in private makeshift jails outside the control of the news Government.

The document seen by The Independent, states that while political prisoners being held by the Gaddafi regime have been released, their place has been taken by up to 7000 new "enemies of the state," "disappeared" in a dysfunctional system, with no recourse to the law.

Nature is forever giving us a chance at what we call rebirth and death, and we in our folly, in our fear of death, fail to understand that which represents a new journey, a new page on which to write, and thus believe in a new beginning for ourselves....
 *The truth is that my body has come to existence, and that it will cease to exist. I am eternal.*Rev. Parthasarathy Rajagopalachari

Nature's law dictates that in order to survive, bees must work together. As a result, they instinctively possess a sense of social responsibility. They have no constitution, no law, no police, no religion, or moral training but, because of their nature, the whole colony survives. We human beings have a constitution, laws, and a police force. We have religion, remarkable intelligence, and hearts with a great capacity to love. We have many extraordinary qualities but, in actual practice, I think we are behind those small insects. In some ways, I feel we are poorer than the bees.

His Holiness the XIVth Dalai Lama

I feel Libyan people should seek
Pursuit of peace, and should stay away
from revenge and warmongering.

HOT NEWS AND WIDE-ANGLE VIEWS

Saif al-Islam offered $Two billion bribe to rebels for his release. "New Libya" to be governed by Islamic Laws-Permitting Polygamy.
Gaddafi's body was never handed over to family as promised?
Russian draft resolution to secure Libyan arms stockpiles.
Chechnya's Kadyrov fears Libya's situation will not improve after Gaddafi.
Muammar Gaddafi made good on his promise to die for Libya and its oil. But NATO, UK, FRANCE, and USA did not.

ICC's verdict on NATO'S war crimes was that "NATO and their collaborators are innocent for their actions in Libya as

119

well as any future conflicts they will initiate around the World." says Kim.

> "Very well paid judges, prosecutors and other staff of ICC are very corrupt, but they are not stupid enough to cut the hand that feeds them." says Boban Djurdjevic.

(Both above are extracted from 18 Comments published in the Middle East news on Nov. 2011.)

Obama says Libyan people can now determine their destiny. I think it is a political baloney, and is poles apart from his use of drones hiding in the Garb of Innocence. *NO ONE WILL EVER FIND OUT HOW EVIL AND SELFISH THE WESTERN INTERVENTION WAS*? However it was a necessary evil to stop Gadhafi's vicious acts of torture and espionage.

USA pledges $40 million to Libya for arms pile up safety. My question is what will they get out of it? Another question is that Bush also gave tons of money personally to Musharif but Pakistani people never got a penny from it?

Britain re-opens Embassy in Tripoli.

Russian energy Ministry hopes new Libyan authority will uphold contract.

Syrian diplomatic mission has been given 72 hours to leave the country stating that our country that has triumphed over the tyranny and dictatorship can only stand by the oppressed.

US missiles killed al-Qeada's chief in Pakistan Badr Mansoor, who sent fighters to Afghanistan and ran a training camp in North Waziristan, in a pre-dawn drone strike.

There is a prevalent theory about the cunning and over indulgent Americans, who are basically hated by the general public. They think USA fooled Gaddafi, by first making him bow down and talked him out of keeping the Weapons of mass destruction, and then planned to kill him, such that all the secret negotiations were buried with him.

@ @ @ @

Variety is the first principle of life.
What makes us formed beings?
"Differentiation."

Perfect balance will be destruction.

Swami Vivekananda

LIBYA'S IMMEDIATE FUTURE?

(For whom does the Bell toll?
What does the melting Pot hold?)

The lawless manner of Muammar el-Gaddafi's death-He was beaten, dragged, sodomised, and shot by a mob of armed men.

Like Mussolini, and Ceauşescu, Gaddafi perished by the same sword that he lived by. We should regret the absence of the fair trial that even the worst criminal deserves, but it's hard not to feel a certain incisive satisfaction at the humiliating and despicable way that one of recent history's genuine monsters passed to his reward.

121

They buried him secretly ignoring a request in the press to NTC to ensure a proper and dignified funeral, befitting a fallen head of state. The contemptuous, hateful, demeaning and downright dirty behavior in the disposal of an enemy's body from which the soul has departed (and he can do no more harm) reflects on the lack of forgiveness and grace of the almighty assassin.

The case in point, is the hanging of Omar Mukhtar, Saddam, serving Assama to the sharks or ocean's man-eaters, by the rebels who are supposed to be the fore-bearers of Libya's bright future? I feel lesser hopeful than I could! It reminds me of a lesson by my GURU when I was 7 years old. He said a tree full of fruit bows down, but the leafless dry branches of a diseased tree stand erect arrogantly!
That said a mob-abetted execution is not exactly the *ideal* way to inaugurate an era of liberty and stability in Libya.
The fact that the interim government couldn't match the already low standard of procedural justice set by Iraq's trial of Saddam Hussain is a reminder of just how far we are from being able to declare a successful end to our North African intervention.

Another point, which will trouble Gaddafi's soul, is the fact that he sent his daughter Aisha to defend Saddam Hussain at his trial and was fervently active in supplying lots of funds and other legal advisors to protect him!
And yet he was treated like a bag of garbage, without any aid or was not judged by any standard rule of law!

The interim leaders are shamefully admitting that the ongoing fighting had prevented them from focussing on other pressing concerns, including the proliferation of armed militias that answer to no central authority.

This unruly free for all, horrible mob rule is worse than, the Long reign of a greedy autocrat.
With the fall of Gaddafi government, neither the administration, nor the rebel leadership has a plan to integrate the former fighters into the new Libyan State.

On 16 September 2011, the U.N. General Assembly approved a request from the National Transitional Council to accredit envoys of the country's Interim Controlling body as Tripoli's sole representatives at the UN, effectively recognizing the National Transitional Council as the legitimate holder of that country's UN seats.

An on-the-ground examination by the New York Times of air strike sites across Libya-including interviews with survivors, doctors, and witnesses, and the collection of remnants of munitions, medical reports, death certificates and photographs-found credible accounts of dozens of civilians killed by NATO in many distinct attacks.

The victims, including at least 29 women or children, who had been *asleep in homes* when the ordnance hit. In all, at least 40 civilians, and perhaps more than 70, were killed by NATO at these sites, as the prevalent evidence suggested. This is just a small random sampling. The gravity of the situation is obvious, because the multi-tonnage bomb explosions can do immeasurable damage with several thousands of innocent victims as happened in World wars, especially when the air attacks can spread over acres. *Most of the evidence gets burnt or destroyed in the explosions.*
There is no chance of protecting the innocent bystanders, or unemployed poor, when the recent rebels have become the rulers. It is a jungle out there and the situation is worsening, and might reach a flash point if immediate action is not taken.

It is like people who break into your house, becoming vigilantes.

While they were bent upon getting rid of the common enemy Gaddafi who was keeping the dirty hands of the greedy west away from country's oil wealth. They were watching closely and forced themselves into the sovereign air space of Libya. Now they have no interest in helping build Libya's future because they rather *divide and rule to serve their greed and need for oil!*

The only saving grace for Libya's Destiny would be if *USA, FRANCE, ITALY, GERMANY AND ABOVE ALL BRITAIN* start fighting with each other; then it will be the story of the monkey and the cats who fought for their share of the cake?

At this moment all the accumulated wealth by Gaddafi in foreign banks was frozen and supposedly distributed to the *NTC*. Also they have done a perfect job of keeping the Libyan Oil flowing!

We hope if *NTC* fails, another strong man like Gaddafi will emerge and create some system out of the currently prevalent horrible chaos.

The minimal tasks for the *NTC* are to establish democratic institutions, strengthening civil society (creating coercion free space between people and the state,) ensuring the rule of law, curbing corruption, maintaining security and facilitating civil and political rights.

Libya did not have any political parties or a social culture. They never experienced any political contest, against a state apparatus.

From here and at this prospectus it will take years to build a working democratic institution, as they experience roadblocks during the transition and several rough learning curves ahead! Eventually the level of success of the transitional phase will determine the prospects for "democratic consolidation," in Libya.

This brings us to the popular opinion of certain wise thinkers that this regional revolution may not spread like a wild fire, in all the ARAB nations and may fade away and fall down by the Fall of 2012. This certainly would help improve the Libyan Destiny, by eliminating the fodder (inspiring, arming and playing on the sentiments of the underdogs) to feed on the western Greed?

Another prediction is that the intelligent youth with a peaceful desire to unite may not exist in large numbers in other Middle East countries? Also majority may not have been caught in the Facebook Web!

Do not forget that western powers are not doing a merciful humanitarian act as do-gooders. They have ulterior motives all the same!

The process of creating a new constitution and a government elected by free and fair voting is dragging on!

On the contrary many of the local militia who helped topple Colonel Gaddafi (or in reality that were helped by *NATO* powers, and the vicious air strikes,) *abandoned a pledge*, to give up their weapons.

They want to preserve their autonomy and influence political decisions as "Guardians of the Revolution."

Where may I ask is the so-called *DEMOCRACY*?

Either way the Pendulum is swinging freely. Like in Iraq, after a decade of war we have made the whole Middle East Zone worse, by our interference and intervention! We the great Democratic Nation have burnt $trillions in fire and smoke, killed the so-called dictator and tyrant, fearing that he may have destroyed us with weapons of mass destruction. We even invented that the Osama-bin-laden had the unique capability, intelligence, and scientific wizardry to attack and destroy our nation, single-handed? What a powerful propaganda machine, the art of hypnosis, to fool the gullible majority. How can a kidney less old man hiding in rugged, inaccessible mountains, ever organize detailed destruction? This inspite of his having intelligent and devoted followers. Bush wasted several thousand tons of bombs and years searching for Osama in inaccessible rugged mountains, while Obama got him in a rich Pakistani neighborhood in the quiet of the night?

I will vote any day for Ron Paul. He has better common sense than many as he rightfully proclaims that we should mind our own business. We must attend to our own economy. We must not waste the hard-earned money of our middle class, by two or more members in each family working over 40 hours a week each. Avoid pushing them down to the poor and unemployed class, by burning our dollars in senseless wars. Remember they are spending our money, which we do not have to start with. Over borrowing to make up the losses in interfering in wars of the Middle East who hate us for doing that and throw old shoes at our President. In comparison Libya, cost us an infinitesimal (hundreds of millions dollars?) However we are obliged to China for their loans, and in turn we have to accept their goods, even thugh it affects our farmers' exports.

"Constitutional Declaration" that after the selection of the new government it would take at least eight months to hold elections for a national assembly is questionable to say the least? What happened to the hundreds of millions spent in the Libyan Arab Spring, each by Britain, Italy, France, Germany, USA + others?

Italian Prime Minister even hosted special dinner to honor Gaddafi and Obama was the first American president who not only greeted Gaddafi, but also sat next to him. Gaddafi also compared him to his son!

Condoleezza Rice, during her visit stayed in Colonel's private abode. Rebels raved about a huge album full of her beautiful photos they found in his bedside drawer. The media and her interview with Piers Morgan brought out two obvious teasers. One was that she felt elated by the glowing praise that was showered on her, for her beauty, with a touch of romantic stance -and she was bathing in that praise like a young girl

126

would do? These are just conjectures through guesswork. I even made a painting of Gaddafi's shy coy, lost-in-love look. He was dressed up like a colorful young bridegroom so to speak!

Excuse me for bringing a lighter humane side, albeit briefly to a shameful, horrible, disastrous subject.

Belgian Weapons in Libya-the Kalashnikovs were clutched at export points and most did not reach Gaddafi's gunmen. Either way they all landed up in rebel hands. This makes the task of integrating former fighters into the Libyan State ever so insurmountable!

Avoiding internal contentious conflict between the present hierarchy is of vital importance. NTC are at the toughest transitional stage of development, and sitting on a heap of cash, forcibly taken from Gaddafi's coffers with NATO' help.

As a result of the civil war of February to October 2011, the Libyan Arab Jamahiriya, which had at that time been in existence for 34 years, collapsed.

Jibril announced that consultations were under way to form an interim government within one month, followed by elections for a constitutional assembly within eight months and parliamentary and presidential elections to be held within a year after that. He stepped down as expected the same day and was succeeded by Ali Tarhouni temporarily.

At least 30,000 Libyans died in the civil war.

They are at a politically critical juncture when their unity against the common enemy who has been eliminated is stretched at seams! Simultaneously *NATO* has lost interest and gone home and are not holding *NTC*'s hands, as soon the Oil started to flow. Everything and everybody who were brought together have wandered off in different directions.

NTC must also address the clear and present danger of:

Further civil unrest and potential tribal-based political discrimination that could undermine democratic elections (in which NTC elite could solicit their favorites to run for top political offices.)

They must also address the ideological and cultural differences between the West (Tripolitania-Tripoli) and East (Cyrenaica-Benghazi,) *TRIPOLI* to bring about national unity. They will be walking a very tight rope to achieve all the above. The most impotant, pressing, and daunting challenge for NTC arguably is to set up solid ground for deliberation on a new and solid Libyan constitution, which will frame the institutional arrangement for the 'new' Libya. Remember Gaddafi controlled with a strong fist, single handedly. Perhaps many *LITTLE GADDAFIS WOULD NOW BE* raising their uglier heads to replace him? A sea of difference exists between the established democracies of this world and the present status and reality in Libya. A big vacuum has been created by the sudden departure of the opposing parties namely Gaddafi and NATO, representing the interfering *WESTERN POWERS*.

WHAT SHOULD LIBYA DO?

BBC's Carolina Hawley, in Tripoli reported (I personally like the BBC's news as the least biased,) that the African Union were concerned. They said, "through the *NATO* and the West we have lost one of our brothers. Muammar Gaddafi won elections and was a true leader. It is foreigners who toppled him not Libyans. Gaddafi died fighting. He is a true African

Hero." The rebels who captured and most likely killed and sodomized him were supported and instructed by *NATO*, yet they refused to hand over his body to *NTC* (depends upon who you believe,) because they do not trust their leader?

They said, "Mahmoud Jibril, ten years close ally of Gaddafi, was imposed upon us by the West, and became a turncoat against Gaddafi! He promised but now refuses to resign." Tensions between the Pro-West groups who worked against Gaddafi are now brewing furiously. The threads of union, which tied them as a well-knit team are now breaking thin, after NATO's departure."

After Gaddafi's assassination, the right thing to do would be for the African Union and the United Nations to convene an International conference on Libya. Libyans from all shades of political divide shall attend this. This shall enable them to agree on a transitional government and programs to move towards a new constitutional, electoral and governance dispensation.

The above mentioned organizations are not strong enough to ensure a resolute outcome if China, Russia and several other countries capable of and ready to provide financial, political and martial aid were beaten in the game by the western nations. The topmost involvement was from America (who borrows money from China,) and France, Germany, and England. This has already caused dissentions in the UN Security Council.

To convene a General Assembly of the UN would need meeting of several minds. This in itself is an impossible task, and may never happen in our lifetime. It is like the divination of the supposed influences of the stars and planets on human affairs and terrestrial events by their positions and aspects.

The resultant benefit of such an ideal conference would be that weapons and soldiers would not be dispersed and later turned into armed bandits and mercenaries who would destabilize the whole region.

With the departure of convoys, from Libya with their arsenal of weapons, it is now becoming obvious that the region must be protected from destabilization and bloodshed. The objective of war is to enforce the will of the combatant over his adversary. Gaddafi was on his way out, as soon as his supporters reached the point of no return, and could not maintain order, nor pursue international relations.

BUILDING A NEW LIBYA!

AU, and UN's failure to stop the timely disintegration of Libya's infrastructure would leave the country unstable for decades to come. It behooves these two international forums to save the day and their face, by calling the above-mentioned International Conference!

The answer to building new Egypt, Libya, and Tunisia is evading us so far. Much less certain are the algorithms that lead to a peaceful ending and successful conclusion of a genuine resolution.

The (?) marks in above few sentences alone are:

Prevalent CORRUPTION, not letting up?

Soaring of food prices, wide spread homelessness, and increasing unemployed, amongst the younger generations, even though these are less prevalent in Libya?

What combination of factors will it take to liberate Libya and having done so, what would be required to turn liberated Libya, Egypt and Tunisia into peaceful, prosperous and democratic nations?

Libya has some advantages over the others, because it is an oil rich country and has a very small population. This is unlike Egypt and Tunisia where the maximum funds were locked up in the coffers of the top dictators, which can be shared, but the future is bleak!

It has higher Sunni population and negligible religious diversity.

The problem in Libya stems from its 140 tribes and clans, some of them with   centuries old enmities.

There's the language divide between the Berber minority and vast Arab-speaking people.

Gaddafi had the practical wherewithal of keeping the two sides at bay to avoid direct conflict. He manipulated sharing high-powered government jobs and kept the two sides happy. He kept them all inline by employing a fine mixture of patronage and punishment.

You see I have mentioned in my other books that there is need of Dictators, as they play a necessary role in keeping warring parties at safe distance because of their authoritative commands. I remember after *TITO* the whole of Yugoslavia could never be united and live in prosperity as they did during his dictatorship.

By the way *TITO* was not his real name. This nickname followed from his strong dictatorial commands. "TI" means you and "TO" means GO, or I might have interchanged the two? Anyway because he was forever ordering people around he was always shouting TI and TO so he earned that nickname.

We lost a useful dictator in killing Saadam Hussain, who kept the Sunnis and Shiia's in their places, instead of hating and killing each other. Also Saadam was the only one who could keep Iran within their borders as the war between them continued for several years. Horrible as they were, Dictators too have a role in the human jungle!

Matching that, but without repression is perhaps the biggest challenge for the NTC. But the rebels can count on economic, military help and political sympathy from Europe and USA. Many NTC members are from the Libyan Diaspora, including several from the US. The designated Finance and Oil Minister, Ali Tarhouni is an ex-teacher from the Washington University where he taught business economics before returning to Benghazi at the start of the rebellion. He will not stay away from his respected job for long!

Western contact will be crucial to Libya's economic prospects. The NTC is pressing governments worldwide to unfreeze more than $100 billion in Gaddafi's assets to help jump-start an economy paralyzed by six months of fighting. Obama has already promised to release frozen funds and provide expert and diplomatic support. Any transition is burdened with political entanglement even if money is freely available. Many western powers would like to keep an eye on controlling the OIL wealth of Libya that may result in political wrangling!

Then there is the convoluted system of "people's committees" which was the media Gaddafi used for supreme personal control of the country. NTC will need to move towards a traditional government. In the meantime there are many vicious wild cats in the jungle out there. How and when would we be able to tame Syria and, bring down its tyrant? Let us not forget the couple of wild Cheetas in Libya, The Eastern Libyans from Benghazi, and the western Berbers from the mountains as well!

The revolutionaries and despots in the rest of the Middle East would be keenly watching, how the next few months phase out. The world is hoping that the monarchies and emirates like Assad of Syria, Ali Abdullah Salah of Yemen, King Saud (who has somewhat loosened his purse strings to the university graduates) in Saudi Arabia shall rise to the occasion?

We have to watch how the elections set up by the interim government in Tunisia, turn out. The Morocco King has already announced constitutional reforms. The unrest in Algeria has temporarily been staved off by pay raises and stabilizing food prices. Lebanon and Israel youth are not sitting at home either!

The "Ace" in the pack of all the above mentioned political hotchpotch is USA. The powers that be (Obama) could change and the new (TEA?) party in power may upset the balance of power all over again? Yet another joker in the pack and another wait and see game? The future remains uncertain. Talking about our country we are no Angels. We go places, interfere in other country's politics and then sit, watch and pass judgements.

The main culprits could possibly be the Drought; the Shería's Law, Famine, TRG similar to *NTC, and lack of central government?* Or America's involvement and Aid as a weapon etc.

A case in point is *Somalia's Famine,* which indirectly was caused by us i.e. US! Our campaign against Islamic terrorists contributed to a catastrophe that continues to kill hundreds of thousands.

Looking at the picture in the September 5, 2011 issue of the TIME Magazine, page 41 " *Misery in Mogadishu,*"

We see soldiers' patrol former al-Shabab territory.

Relatives prepare a seven yr. old, Umar Usman for burial; Women await medical treatment; Mothers watch over their dead and dying children, and much more.

By June and July their goats were all gone, and the last of their cows sank to their knees and died. People with their rags, some plastic bottles, and cooking pots marched to Mogadishu on foot 155 miles to the east. At every village they passed, their groups grew, first to columns of hundreds, then thousands, and then tens of thousands, as millions across southern Somalia abandoned their homes. With little water and only leaves to eat, the young and old quickly perished. Bagey Ali, who walked 185 miles from Qansax Dheere, saw seven people "just sit down and die." When his children started fading on the 310-mile trek to Baoli Bishar, 60 years of age carried them on his shoulders. When he realized they were dead, he buried them on the way, loosing three boys and two girls that way.

A mass exodus, an emptying of half a country, is an unprecedented, biblical event. Drought is the immediate and primary cause. The rains failed last October and again April this year. UN was putting the population at risk from hunger in Djibouti, Ethiopia, Eritrea, Kenya, Somalia and Uganda at 12.4 million. The number of Somali children with severe acute malnutrition-near death was 170,000, of which 29,000 had already died. There is no chance of preventing

100,000+ Somalis, from dying in the next few weeks. How did this happen? How is that millions of Somalis were so sure that no help was coming that they took their families on a death march across the scorching desert? The answers reveal how a war between Islamic militants and the U.S. and its allies led directly to human catastrophe. UN Food and Agriculture Organization says this year's drought is the worst since 1950-51 and the successive rain failures mean an area the size of France has become desert in 60 years. But drought just sets the condition for famine; only man ensures it. Somalis have been fighting one another and have lived without a central government, for 20 years.

The U.S. is the key international player. Few Americans have set foot in Mogadishu, since the 1993 battle known as the Black Hawk Down, when 18 U.S. troops died, during an intervention to support a UN mission in an earlier famine. But the U.S. has assassinated several Islamist leaders inside Somalia, using Predator drones, cruise missiles fired from war ships and, once a helicopter gun ship. Also the U.S. bankrolled the TFG that had not even been elected into power!

Aid as a Weapon

By LATE 2009 THE U.S. WAS WITHHOLDING
about $50 million in food aid from al-Shabab territory.
By early 2010 the U.S. was in a standoff with aid
workers, requiring them to refuse to pay the toll al-
Shabab demanded, if they wanted U.S. funding. For its
part, al-Shabab expelled the World Food Program
(WFP) in January 2010, calling it an U.S. proxy. On its
narrow terms, U.S. strategy succeeded. Al-Shabab has
been severely weakened by a combination of famine
and the loss of Middle Eastern funding since the
political turmoil there. On Aug. 6 2010 it withdrew
from Mogadishu. But what impoverished al-Shabab's
few thousand fighters also helped push a few million
Somalis to the brink of starvation. The same areas that
were ruled by al-Shabab are now blighted by famine.
On the ground in those regions are the Red Cross,
several Islamic charities, a handful of Médecins sans
FrontièresWorkers and UNICEF contractors, The
WFP, the giant famine relief set up, whose slogan is
"Fighting hunger world wide." is absent. The UN says
just 20% of the 2.8 million southern Somalis in need are

being reached. "The famine is proof of U.S. success," says Tony Burns, operations director for the Somali aid group Saacid. IF THERE IS LITTLE AID I THE FAMINE areas, there is not enough outside them. The WFP was distributing 85,000 hot meals a day through local charities, a small fraction of what Mogadishu's 500,000 refugees needed.

BACK TO LIBYA

After forcing Libya's Air force from its own sovereign air space, NATO countries continued the ritual of daily (day and night,) bombardment of innocent civilians, children, women whom they were trusted to protect from Gaddafi's airplanes attacks.

Gaddafis of this world were no match for the drones secretly aimed at them with pinpoint accuracy. At the end of the callous foreign invasion, over two hundred thousand civilians out of a total population of 2.5 million were killed defenselessly!
Was it wise of NTC to have invited foreign military invaders especially NATO, to land cruise missiles and bombs from the air and ground aimless on their citizens and destroy their infrastructure, which Gaddafi belabored for 42 years to build? Gaddafi was never a saint, and he stayed far too long? But where was UN AND NATO when Julius Nyerer of Tanzania ruled for 25 years; Felix Houphouet-Boigny of Cote D'Ivoire for 14 years; Kenneth Kaunda of Zambia ruled for 27 years (1964-91); Uganda's Yoweri Museveni since 1986 to date; Zimbabwe's Robert Mugabe from 1980 to date. Indonesia's

Suharto reigned for 30 years, Korea's Kim II for 46 years and Cuba's Castro (+ his Brother) are still going strong as always.

As long as there is division in any form there must be conflict. You are responsible, not only to your children, but also to the rest of humanity. Unless you deeply understand this, not through words or ideas or the intellect, but feel this in your blood, in your way of looking at life, in your actions, you are supporting organized murder, which is called war.

Krishnamurti

+++++

In the song of the rushing torrent,
Hold on to the joyful assurance:
I will become the sea.
And this is not a vain supposition;
It is absolute humility, because it is the truth.

Rabindranath Tagore

{{{{{{

Your way is very good for you, but not for me.
My way is good for me, but not for you.

Swami Vivekananda

The Libyan Conundrum

To my simple mind the difference is that the country has massive desert full of hundreds of nomads and tribes living in far-flung places in the rough and dry areas. They are self-sufficient.

Gaddafi directly controlled the army and ammunition. He ensured that no one was armed and possessed bullets.

He had established direct contact between himself and every Libyan through his political spies as the sole proprietor, the sole congressman, sole guru of the ordinary man on the street. This is possible because 78% population lives in the seven coastal towns, which he constantly pays, surprise visits to.

He was the world's experienced leader in espionage, counter espionage, and murders. Everyone, who knew this, hated him and called him a madman.

He ruled the country by a networking of spooks and snitchers, as you can read elsewhere in my other publications-Please visit my web site for that:

www.authorgopalbooks.com

Irrespective of these differences, he had been overtaken by a new and unstoppable, frustrations of the new youth, and new tools generated by advancement in technology e.g. the social media like Facebook, cell phones, satellite communications, I-pods, I-phones, computers etc. which he could not fight! Up till now he had given out Radios, TV sets and installed antennas free for his people and had ensured that they tune into, energized Transmitters (I could never get CNN on my system there) 24x7.

Gaddafi consistently and constantly kept alive his propaganda that ensured his praises and sermons continuously, same as the Reverend Jones did to his faithfuls in Jones town massacre! The big difference in Gadaffi's regime was its similarity to Castro and its ruthlessness towards political opponents.

He killed about 1300 inmates in 1996 at Abu Salim prison after a riot sparked by appalling conditions, as per Hashim Matar who is about to publish his book "Anatomy of a Disappearance."

For 15 years the regime had been refusing to give out the names of the killed or return their bodies for respectful burials by their loved ones. Those who challenged the official version of suppressing the massacre ended up in Abu Salim just like Fathi Terbill who had agreed to represent the families. A group of lawyers and judges had gathered in front of Benghazi's main courthouse to protest. The victim's families joined them and the demonstration grew into a full-blown rebellion that resulted in liberating eastern Libya from Gadaffi's grips, and finally toppled him from Tripoli as well.

On the other side of that war from Al-Tahawy was Major Ahmad Mahmud, one of Gaddafi's die-hard loyalists. After the rebellion broke out in the east, he was part of a contingent sent

144

to try to retake the town of Al-Baida. They fought for days around the airport but the rebels killed 120 Gadaffi supporters. Gadaffi, commonly called a madman in the western world pointed to the words inscribed on Libya's Central Bank brick exterior "The Authority and the revolution and the weapons are in the hands of the people." But don't forget he was talking about his revolution when he dethroned King Sanussi, and when he was one of the people! Now he was the tyrant!

On the issue of sanctions recommended by the United Nations and the request of the oppressed people for arms and financial aid, there had been a feeble response from US. But the good news is that as per General Abdulrahman Fadah Abdulrahman "Every Libyan now has a gun- including old people, women, and those who don't, will be given one. We are confident of the outcome, he announced."

Obama opposed the implementation of "No FLY Zone." that tantamount to a war? So NATO forces dropped several Tomahawk missiles, costing a $million/per bomb (on material cost only)- to neutralize Gaddafi's Airpowers considerably. This had built up some support for the revolt against Gaddafi by his people.

On the other hand his life size images are embedded in the windscreens of private cars, Cell phones. Also people walking or resting in the park carry Gaddafi's Photo. As I have already explained in this chapter, why he chose to give himself the title of Colonel. He loved to think that he was the popular "Old Brother"- Leader of the Libyan masses. He proclaimed he was not a King, Sultan, and not even a President.

He could never tolerate NTC making weapons available to the masses for direct use against him. Therefore he heaped Misery on Misratah in a Ding-dong battle! The rebels' complained that NATO was slipping from their promised mission. The reality was that most nations including USA were over committed on several fronts, perhaps aimlessly! Simultaneously there was an all round economic desperation and nature's fury was beating

145

the willpower of the Japanese people. Obama had lots of embarrassments and pressures. The Chinese ditched him. The Iranians ditched him. The corrupt nonentities like Afghanistan's Hamid Karzi defied him. He was double-dealt by the Pakistanis. And recently he has been criticized for mishandling the Arab Spring revolutions by pussy footing. Quoting Pete Souza, the transcript of his phone calls to Mubarak a close USA ally, showed that his way of a directive asking him to step down was firm, full of civilities but no threats, but no give-in either. Another guy could have been rough, direct and loud but his was more effective and grandfatherly! E.g. he said, " I have no interest in embarrassing you. I want to help you secure your legacy by ushering in a new era."

Gadhafi on the other hand said I am ready to talk to Obama. *He is like my son!*

But Obama's indulgence in Libya's humanitarian cause might have been muscled through by a coterie of female policy advisors, a little tougher than he was! I can fill another 200 pages with incoherent quotes and daily changing stories but will end by saying that the Libya's situation is in a STALEMATE. I personally think Obama is doing OK! It is more important to arrive at a smart policy than to start shooting first and ask questions later. In the Osama Bin Laden's case, he has done well on two-counts

He saw through Pakistan's treachery when he became President. You would have easily seen this from certain of his remarks when he took over. Killing Osama, dumping his body in the ocean secretly could win him a second term, but the after-taste will be felt later. Questions that may be asked are: What if Muslims glorify Osama as a martyr, like Lord Christ?

The Middle-East Conundrum

Over the millennium several phenomenal changes took place in our universe. Some of these were in the equatorial regions south of the Mediterranean Ocean.

With the upheavals generated by earthquakes and other ferocious ocean moves Sahara became a barren land thousands of miles inland from the most colorful and breathtaking ocean with picture-perfect interplay of dozens of Green and Blue hues of ocean waves.

Before these major shifts it was easy to rule several countries simultaneously. This resulted in the formation of the Roman, Greek, British, Russian, and French, empires to name a few. With the vast spread of aridization of the continent the Middle East became a huge desert where it was impossible to travel and or live without vegetation. Smaller villages cropped up along the coastal areas having Goats and Camels as their worldly possessions.

With the discovery of oil, the advancement of science and technology, the development of the Automobile, Diesel Engines, and machines, countries needed oil to run them. The demand of developing countries for oil encouraged them to develop technologies like drilling and methodology to extract gas from the hidden layers of mother earth. Soon came the Manufacturing industries that build weapons and tools of transportation, and some times war.

Hence oil rich belt of small emirates (rich folks) E.g. Bahrain, Saudi Arabia, Abu Dhabi, Kuwait and many more cropped up. They were all based on the model of ruling Sheikhs. The western countries that were their clients and technicians befriended these little empires.

The Islam religion, which was based on the principle of socio-economic, was spontaneously successful and widely spread. The prime reason for hundred percent acceptances was that this religion had zero discrimination. They were all brothers – sons of Allah and drank from the same common pot, smoked from one common hookah, ate from the same heap by sitting around a common fire pit, as one big happy family.

Only in later years it split into two factions. *Shiias* were followers of Ali and the Imams, as the only rightful successors of Muhammad and *Sunnis* who followed the orthodox belief that the first four caliphs were the rightful successors of Muhammad.

A few of Ali's partisans orchestrated the murder of the third Caliph Uthman in 656AD, and Ali was named Caliph. Ali in turn was assassinated in 661 AD. Ali's son Hasssan (d. 670 AD) is also revered by Shiite Muslim, some of whom claim he was the Sunni caliph Muawiyeh. Ten to fifteen percent of the Muslim population follows the Sunni branch; the balance follows the Shiite Islam.

There are four schools of Sunnis jurisprudence.

Hanafi: Founded in Iraq. It is prevalent in Turkey, Central Asia, the Balkans, Iraq, Syria, Lebanon, Jordan, Afghanistan, Pakistan, India, and Bangladesh.

Maliki: Widely followed in North Africa, Mauritana, Kuwait, and Bahrain.

Shaf'i: Spread in Egypt, Sudan, Ethiopia, Somalia, and parts of Yemen, Indonesia, and Malaysia.

Hanbali: It is prevalent in Saudi Arabia, Qatar, parts of Oman, and the United Arab Emirates.

Scholar Wahhab (1703-1791AD) encouraged a return to the orthodox practice of the " fundamentals" of Islam. In the eighteenth century the founder of the modern-day Saudi dynasty formed an alliance with Wahhabs and unified the disparate tribes in the Arabian Peninsula. The most conservative interpretations of Wahhabi Islam view Shiites and other non-Wahhabi factions as dissident heretics. Following the 1979 Soviet invasion of Afghanistan and the Shiite Islamic revolution in Iran, Saudi Arabias Sunni Ruling royal family began promoting Wahhabi religious doctrine abroad. They have financed the construction of *WAHHABI-ORIENTED MOSQUES, RELIGIOUS SCHOOLS, AND ISLAMIC CENTERS IN DOZENS OF COUNTRIES.*
As Shiites increasing lost their political battles with Sunni Muslim rulers, they were convinced that after the lineage of Imams descended from Ali ended the religious leaders known as mujtahids gained the right to interpret religious, mystical, and legal knowledge to the broader community.

The most learned amongst these teachers are known as ayatollahs (literally-The sign of God.")

When the revolutionaries in Iran pulled down the Shah of Iran-the king who played the British tune, Ayatollah Khoemeni took over.

The Iraq/Iran never ending war was interrupted unwittingly by Bushes (Father and Son.)

I wish USA learned the reality in the Middle Eastern countries and acted statesman like instead of blindly supporting Israel and creating more ill will.

If Republicans take the White House, the swing of the Pendulum will hurt twice: Once because the present President will not have a chance to promote his policy long enough and secondly because the next guy will uproot the good work done to date.

WHAT IS LIBYA'S FUTURE

POST GADDAFI?

The demeaning, uncouth way Gaddafi's final derogatory
Sodomy was video taped by the lowest kind of humans,
I must say has lowered Libya's image, much lower than Gaddafi
could have ever been accused of, in the eyes of the world.

Gaddafi achieved Libya's independence from King Idris
without firing a single shot or publicly demeaning him. He
whipped up the sentiment of ten of his army colleagues,
virtually single-handed.

The present rebellion, if you must call it that was an
opportunistic uprising started off with bayonets until funded by
NATO and eventually by tax payers like you and me, because
America has learnt not to save but to borrow till doomsday.

NATO is not as stupid as the Libyans who eventually would end up loosing their Black Gold through the Wheels and Deals they wound up in, by the *USA, LONDON, AND FRANCE TO START WITH.*

WESTERN NATIONS COULD NOT BROWBEAT GADDAFI HENCE THEY DECIDED TO DISPOSE HIM IN A WAY THAT THE SECRET AGREEMENTS BETWEEN THEM & HIM WERE BURIED WITH HIM.

SAIF, GADDAFI'S SON WILL ALSO BE ASSASSINATED SO HE CANNOT REVEAL THE SECRETS ARRANGEMENTS THEY HAD WITH THE WEST.

The unifying factor within the many diverse factions within Libya (tribal and historic) was the shared hatred and united desire to be rid of Gaddafi. Now that common enemy is gone the pent-up hatred will be redirected against one another in the inevitable ensuing power struggle.
Iraq achieved its purpose and freedom, as seen by Bush cronies but look what is still happening there years after Saddam Hussain's demise. It was he who said that "the revolution chooses its own enemies", yet it was he alone who kept the peace there although, conversely, this was achieved by oppressive means.

So how will Libya's freedom, found by the superpower intervention and unquenchable thirst for oil/gas and other valued resources inextricably entwined with it, help the Libyans?

Will *NATO MEMBERS* ultimately make the Libyan people pay up for such seemingly altruistic acts of benevolence?

WHO WILL NOW SEEK RECOMPENSE FOR THE COST OF BOMBING THE COUNTRY TO THE POINT OF OBLIVION and killing many of the citizens (including innocent women and children) citing such acts as the unfortunate but inevitable results of 'war' and 'collateral damage' by friendly fire?

The whole Universe is to us the writing of the infinite in the language of the finite.

Swami Vivekananda

<u>EAST IS</u> *Middle-***<u>EAST</u>** *with Arab Spring in vogue, and* **<u>WEST IS</u>** *"USA &* **<u>WEST</u>** *Europe" with economic woes - we are told.* **<u>THE TWAIN</u>** *shall* **<u>MEET</u>** *at gas geysers and wells of liquid gold.*

US Defense Secretary arrives in Afghanistan to meet with commanders. Panetta will also visit *IRAQ, LIBYA*, and *TURKEY*. He will be the first Pentagon Chief to visit Libya. He said that USA would take time to determine how to help the new government.
Graffiti thanks U.S. for role in ousting Gaddafi.
What have we come to? A great nation is being thanked through Graffiti —the language of the Gangs in America.

153

Of course America will have to sort out with the other Western Allies and not so friendly nations how much share of the oil loot comes their way. Also it will take years to settle the new politics of the land to confirm how cooperative the new Government becomes. It took decades to befriend and/or win the *SANNUSI* kings as the British and American puppets! French foreign Minister pledges to work with other UN Security Council members to unfreeze remaining Libyan assets. Spain's oil giant Repsol resumes pumping oil in Libya. BP says it wants to do the same.

UK Defense Secretary Phillips Hammond confirms cost of British operations in Libya as £212 million.

THERE WILL BE FRANCE, GERMANY, ITALY AND EVER SO MANY others who will roll in and put their hands out to share the Black Liquid Gold,

THEY could not get this cheap when Gaddafi was keeping them at bay. That was the prime and solitary reason to assassinate and silence him. They referred to him, as the madman of the Middle East because they were mad at him and just could not stand up to him. If he were not so lucky he would have been eliminated over 30 years ago! But when he showed some cooperation the Bush gang befriended him, the main objective is always to grab the Oil riches one way or the other. As they say in Indian language, which when translated literally means *"The elephant has two types of teeth, one for showing off and others for eating."*

The relationship between Egypt and Libya worsened recently and the open border between the two countries over the centuries is now closed.

Gaddafi's soul would indeed be restless to discover this turn of event when his main objective was to unify Africa and there was an open border between the two good neighbors except when Sadat opposed Gaddafi and befriended the West and Israel!

How little the past and potential future Presidents know about the Middle East is obvious from the blatant remarks by the presidential candidate for Republicans Herman Cain who suggested that most of the US Muslims were extremists. He also stumbled badly on Libya question. Campaign says he was on 4 hours sleep. It took him that long to recall the specifics. Rival militias agreed on truce after 4 days of fighting.
I wonder if they were tired, of awaiting help from NATO superiors or were plain drunk?
M16 thwarted suicide car bomb plot to kill Western diplomats, as per a senior NTC member in Libya!
Libya leaders appeal to UN again to unfreeze funds.
I personally believe that they would need a nod from the main bosses USA, UK, FRANCE, ITALY, GERMANY, and others. These countries in turn will use this opportunity to soften up the new Government that replaced Gaddafi to get the bargains to possess the liquid Gold at lowest prices. It is a "wait and see" game.
Recent bits of news crossing the wires:

Drone attacks have been intensified in Waziristan lately, Libyan army head may be the next target for assassination, by the same tools. Qatar admits it had boots on the ground in Libya! They have been meddling, a lot lately in various neighboring Arab states encouraging Muslim fundamentalists and channeling money and arms discreetly to these protestors. The Prime Minister Abdel Rahim el-Keeb appointed the militia's commander to be the new defense minister. He actually bowed down to the local militia holding Seif al-Islam el-Gaddafi as a prisoner.
This gives yet another glimpse of the possible future outcome? My conviction based on the historical facts is that several Middle Eastern countries with divergent tribal content lend themselves to be led by a single leader who shows them the fist.

Gaddafi pumped both fists in the air. They are like sheep that need a shepherd.

A group of leaders can never conform to a comprehensive whole, like a single *"ONE MAN SHOW"* can!

Check out the history of Egypt/Tunisia/Syria/Iraq/Yugoslavian and several other countries.

Arab Spring, movement started in Arab speaking countries and so far as we can judge from the current events it has not been successful?

In Egypt the army supported the cause of the HAVE-NOTS, and now they are raping the freedom fighting women instead of standing against the regime supporters. It is a massive desert out there, covered with Storms and Sand!

In Libya so far the Storm is brewing and the peace and calm albeit under the strong fist of the despot Gaddafi, has been sandblasting!

Even with the democracy established for hundreds of years the two parties in control in *USA, UK* keep *"YO-YO ING"* like Pendulum Swings.

At the very best it will take years not months to pave a solid road for democratic consolidation. With the reality setting in and discovering the inside truth of the Allies' misuse of the newly gained scientific intelligence, USA's Hegemony over the world can soon become all encompassing.

TOO MUCH POWER IN ONE HAND leads to *Dictatorship*

This is one of the reasons why my faith in Libya's Destiny has to be revisited, *RESTUDIED AND RESEARCHED CONTINUOUSLY!*

FANTASIZING FRAGILE

FUTURE IN LIBYA

During the first six months of the evolution of the Arab spring, I was sure that Gaddafi and Bashar of Syria were capable of suppressing the uprising, which started in Egypt, if it spills over to their shores.

So in my chapter on "Libya's destiny" in my Book " Gaddafi Up- Close," I was full of guts and faith in Libya's Destiny. I was actually proud of my judgement of the circumstances prevailing in Libya. I was indeed sure that my predictions of this country's future under the strong dictatorship of Gaddafi would not be out of line especially when he had mended his ways and was helping the Bush presidency. It was a historical first that the Secretary of State of USA, had historical meetings in Gaddafi's residence. If the facial expressions of Dr. Rice and Gaddafi are any indication it was my judgement that USA will support Libya in the future.

I LIST BELOW SOME OF THE DANGEROUS NEW CLOUDS THAT ARE GATHERING ON THE NEW HORIZON:

Total contempt of democracy on the lines of what happened with Iraq Oil, could repeat in Libya!

Country ripped by Tribal Factions could drift apart and be tempted to offer awards to the States whose bombs helped them to gain power temporarily. These gangs are holding on to the ill-gotten arms and weapons of mass destruction tightly and dearly.

Frittering away Libya's Oil wealth by secret pacts with London based coalition, who assassinated and silenced Gaddafi and will silence his son Saif in the future to bury the
ARM-LENGTH UNDERSTANDINGS REACHED WITH THE GADDAFIS ON THE WORD-OF-HONOR BASIS"
Now that the only guy who could keep the willful grabbers at bay has been sent to an unknown grave, they will make triple or more gains misusing the newly gained "Authority to Loot!"
The elimination of the dictator may bring about several little Gaddafis who may split the country into little unmanageable fragments. This may blow away any hopes of Lady Destiny ever blessing Libya's future?
What comes to my mind is the history repeating itself.
Remember nothing good came out of splitting Yugoslavia into self-destroying pieces. This disunited country is still disintegrating due to revengeful hatred and resulting in massive Genocide and cross fighting. Tito had kept the fighting cats under strict control, and avoided the catastrophic outcomes.

Saddam Hussain was much more useful for Iraq, because he kept the warring religions (Sunnis vs. Shiias) under control. The selfish Mullahs intentionally flared their hatred in the Madrassas.

In the case of Libya there was no religious disharmony and Gaddafi was aggressively trying to unite neighboring African countries. He also kept at bay the freeloading western nations from interfering and forcibly grabbing his country's oil wealth. *Once again convincing me honestly that the Dictators are A Necessary Evil, till they get addicted to greed and reach mental degradation, depravity, and deprivation.*

If Saddam Hussain and Iranians were to continue the longest war based on the Sunni/Shiias factions; America would have continued manufacturing and supplying them Airplanes, Machine Guns, tanks, and war materials. We would have saved $trillions, instead of burning $s in smoke in the wars, not to belittle the loss of our war heroes. We could be sitting pretty and watching all the squabbles between the three Axis of evil!

Hitler's was another completely stand alone unique case of self destruction due to the following events:

A case of JEWS (HAVES), as they AMASSED all the wealth in a few GREEDY hands and left the huge percentage of Germans at below poverty levels.

Hitler led the majority homeless, helpless and hungry (*HAVE-NOTS*), in a popular crusade against the Jews. He soon became a Führer with supreme powers because of unflinching support of the grateful anti-Semitic public.

However the massive power went into Hitler's head and he became senseless, mad, uncontrollable, and derisory.

BRITISH & JAPANESE RUTHLESS MARAUDERS
In their times of glory were merciless and overwhelmed with obedience to the (*KINGS/QUEENS/EMPERORS.*)

159

The ego of Japan in attacking a sleeping Giant USA resulted in their being taught a lesson by *TRUMAN'S DEVASTATING ATOM BOMBS.*

While the Brits used to boast about the fact that the sun never sets on the British Empire- now it rarely rises even in Britain.

IRAN

(*Pride vs. Statesmanship*)

The situation could worsen only if the international community is unable to produce an intelligent statesman. They may become hot headed & unwilling to look for the reality or may be overcome with false pride. Also Iranians may fall prey to the devastating power of overconfidence and religious hegemony of the Ayatollahs. Trying to save a "pawn of self pride" they may receive the crushing defeat of a checkmate.

There are a few evil warmongers amongst the Tea party who want the gullible amongst the richest American Jews to pump in money to the coiffures of Israel. They want Israel instead of *NATO*, to take out Assad. They do not want a democratic or humane government but a pro-USA government there. And after Syria, they want Israel to attack Iran. Israel could really take on all its neighbors and become the Commander-in-Chief of the whole Middle East?

Watching the collapse of Russia 20 years ago and the ease with which they are popping out so many Middle Eastern leaders quietly, USA knows that they are the single power left in the world. So they would like to overthrow China (after manipulating India in the East and Israel in the Middle East to be their quarterbacks in those areas, and frontline fighters in the artillary during regional wars.) Such a cozy and disarming feeling has built up an overconfidence, new hopes, and aspirations that some went as far as to predict that Arab Spring would spread all over the world. But my gut feel and abundant experience with world travels tells me that an overdose of pride can make them blind to the smoldering embers in various suppressed fires of the world that are awaiting just a whiff of air to re ignite the fires of hatred against USA.

EGYPT
(Islamic Brotherhood vs. Arab Spring)

The original success of the Arab spring revolution by the unemployed and scientifically advanced youth using their I phones and other modern Apps was possible because their Egyptian Army relatives also went against the Hosni Mubarak regime.

The later flare-ups of the protests by mobs gathered in the central square, has been evoked by one of the following:

The very army personal managing prison cells became sex fiends and raped, and tortured freedom fighter females. An American reporter had personally experienced free for all, mass raping by dozens in the public square. She nearly died. There was a public display of rage and multiple killings by opposing football-team supporters in the TAHRIR square.

The flash point is so low that 16 Americans, have been charged with illegal cash smuggling and evading Income tax, while working for three non-governmental organizations. USA has currently threatened to cut off larger portion of the $1.55 billions annual aids package if they continue with the present trial against American citizens.

The four generations of Egyptian presidents came from the Armed forces which seems to be strongly supporting Muslim Brotherhood against USA. Human Rights workers are openly spying, and sowing unrest in Egypt. The Egyptian Government has recently turned down IMF loans, and present available funds in the treasury have declined to $10 million, compared to the last year's holdings of $36 million.

<u>OBAMA – The Cool Dude</u>

My faith and hopes for the prospects of a brighter future for Libya dwindled the way Middle East Peace process suffered the wild swings of the pendulum between the Obama and Bush Presidencies.

The super secretive & scientific handling of foreign affairs by the Obama regime included but was not limited to the following:

He sided with Robert Gates on the Libya policy as follows:
Enforcing No-Fly zones is equivalent to declaration of war. and
Security Council's approval is not a license to kill Gaddafi &
Family, nor it is to bomb blast his home & hearth.
But simultaneously and secretly progressed the plans to replace
Gates with Leon Panetta?

Obama secretly coordinated with NATO and encouraged
France, UK, and NTC to go all out to blast and bombard with
Tomahawk missiles, from formidable heights knowing fully
well that these can never be delivered with pinpoint accuracy
and the innocent children, and unarmed civilians minding their
own business, do become victims of unintended consequences.
I was unable to catch up with the super speed with which
Panetta and Obama were playing the "*BANG BANG*" game
like spoiled cowboys. They continued to utilize the
advancement in sciences of *DRONES, MIDGET ROBOTS,
AND* pinpoint *ACCURACY OF THE Google mapping techniques.*
They were helped by the secret swat team, that have become
experts in destroying damaged drones or sophisticated
equipment, to avoid technology secret falling into wrong hands.
These successes resulted in serving Osama to the sharks and
Gaddafi to the shameless rebels who stooped lower than the
victim in every which way.
Cool Cat Obama was intelligently tight lipped. But the crude
republicans, including John McCain shouted from the rooftop
that Obama is pussyfooting, gutless and sweet lipped with all
Axes of Evil countries!
They all want to remove him from the White House so they
could revive their *WAR MONGERING* policies. In the
meantime Obama and his cowboy Panetta and Swat group kept
going all hawk like gangbusters popping off the wanted
criminals in the game of hide and seek from their quiet sky
drones. They just sent two more Al Qaida's most wanted to the

unknown, and untraceable graves where there are no heavenly virgins waiting for them.

This really top class strategy, which is worth admiring, is the fact that Obama's presidency ensures that none of the assassinated victims can become heroes or martyrs. Obama is using his brain not brawn!

Obama is profiting from a Romney advisor Kagan's theory about American Power. Robert Kagan's book is more charitable towards the President. He cheered Obama as he kept the tradition of America's Presidents who have understood America's special role in the world. Obama has killed Osama, neutralized al-Qaeda and toppled Gaddafi. Besides his foreign secretary Clinton has hired Victoria Nuland, who is married to Kagan as her spokeswoman.

Castro called the Republican Primaries as "The greatest competition of idiocy and ignorance that has been."-Sounds hilarious to say the least.

While I was pouring my thoughts in these pages, Mr. Breziznsky, the National security advisor under President Jimmy Carter's Administration was relating his views on the TV. He said " Listening to the debates between the four Republican candidates, he honestly felt deeply embarrassed to be an American." "They are openly showing the rest of the world that their definition of democratic freedom is to remove the Government supervision without which capitalism can never work." he added. And it is a fact that during Carter's presidency Americans were hated lesser than now!

USA will revert back to the Wild West days of the Gold Rush, of the survival of the fittest, and the tyranny of the few rich getting filthy rich by use of unrestricted force and buying desperados to kill any resistance, jut like Gaddafi did till he was assassinated.

He said that through these debates they are telling the rest of the world of what they would do if they take over the White House. It is an open show of brute force against ARAB

SPRING, and blatant disregard of the spread of popular democracy of the unemployed poor majority of the whole world against the 10% rich. Most of the candidates profess support for ZERO taxation for the top one percentage richest, because they obtained their riches the hard way. They earned it. This is the wrong time for Americans to propagate the dual theories, which clash with other countries and send the wrong message. One the one hand they wasted several $millions in Tomahawks to support rebels to assassinate Gaddafi and feeding the coiffures of the *NTC* in Libya. On the other hand they are proposing from the rooftop that the only way to bring democracy is to make the 1% rich, filthy rich. Their idea of reducing the ballooning deficit by eliminating taxes from the richest shows that they do not know how to add and subtract. On the contrary eliminating taxes for top rich and spending on essential programs to reduce the misery of the middle class getting unemployed and poorer will raise the deficit + interest on it.

Gaddafi's recently wrote that the Western powers want to do to Libya what they did to Iraq and what they are itching to do to Iran. They want to take back the oil, which was nationalized, by these countries revolutions. This will double the income of oil companies like Exxon from the present $billions/day. They want to re-establish military bases that were shutdown by the revolutions and to install client regimes that will subordinate Libya's wealth and employment of middle class to imperialist corporate interests. All else is lies and deception. The Gold bullion held by the Libyan Central Bank (March 2011) was amongst the 25 largest reserves in the world. This provided Libya a critical lifeline after billions of Libya's assets was seized by USA and 27 member states of the European Union. Another Libya's well kept secret was Gaddafi's idea to produce a single African currency made from Gold. Here is the reason why he was targeted. There were two conferences on this subject in 1986 and 2000, organized by Gaddafi. Most countries in Africa were keen. This would have eradicated $ and Euro as African currencies.

Hence NATO's keen desire to shut off Gaddaf's mouth. Gaddafi also blasted off the contradictory claims of the NTC that he crippled the education of children to keep them illiterate. On the contrary he propagated that Libya had no external debts and literacy increased from 25% to 87% during his 42 years of reign.

NATO should face War Crimes inquiry over civilian deaths, but western power blocks may manipulate and stop it! It has been a long term American goal to occupy the strategic crossroads between the Mediterranean and the Arab world. Future invasion of Africa by allied forces is imminent, since the land locked and oil rich Uganda provides the ideal location for a permanent U.S. Military base on the African continent to ensure its stranglehold on Central Africa's hydrocarbon and other mineral resources. Congo and Southern Sudan are rich in diamonds, gold, platinum, lithium, and cobalt.

If a man does not of his own free will put himself last amongst his creatures, there is no salvation for him.

Mahatma Gandhi

@@@@@

To go from opinion to perception,

From imagination to fact,

From illusion to reality,

From something not there, to something that is.

That is the way forward.

Swami Prajnanpad

LIBYA'S GEOGRAPHY
AND TOURIST ATTRACTIONS

On our travels from Brega Oil Project towards Tripoli, we proceeded further to Sebratha, only one of many Roman ruins along the Libyan coast. Stunning, amazing, grand, monumental are not adequate to describe my first impressions of Sebratha. The Romans were here at "Tripolitania" after knocking off the Carthaginians at what is now Tunis, about 2,100 years ago.

SEBRATHA, Roman Ruins

Few tourists, other than locals and some sanction opponents have seen these beautiful stone carved structures since the Colonel took command. I was familiar with the Coliseum at El Jem, Dougga, and Carthage in Tunisia, but Sebratha was even better as Roman ruins go.

While Sebratha took my breath away, the first glimpse of Leptis Magna was even more stunning. What a sophisticated city from 200 AD or so. This was an administrative center with some 20,000 residents. It was artistic architecture in stone. The social facilities included stone paved streets, grand theaters, residential areas, market areas, bath houses, brothels, slave quarters and designated channels to remove waste. The adjacent small port had accommodated the sail powered and rowed watercraft that transported grain, wool, hides, olive oil, dates, timber, trade goods, and passengers across the Roman Empire.

The mosaic flooring still remaining in many buildings represented the scope of Roman commerce: different colored stone pieces from the upper Nile, from Tunisia, Algeria, and the quarries around Italy and Sicily.

On our way to Leptis Magna, we passed a large corral area containing many young camels. I was told that this area was a slaughterhouse to provide meat to shops in the city. Camel was often on the menu. I only tried it once.

Tourism in Libya is an industry still in its infancy but one that is gradually growing. There were 1,000,000-day visitors in 2008. The country is best known for its ancient Greek and Roman ruins and Sahara desert landscapes. There are currently about 13,000 Hotel rooms in Libya, a figure the government hopes to increase to 50,000.

Libya can be visited as part of an organized tour, or on a transit visa, obtainable in either Cairo or Tunis.

Archeological Sites

Libya's biggest draw, as a tourism destination is **cultural tourism.** There are five UNESCO World Heritage Sites in the country, three of which are classical ruins. The Roman cities of Sabratha and
Leptis Magna in Western Libya and the Greek ruins of Cyrene in the East are the biggest attractions.

Roman Sites

The theatre at Leptis Magna

The Roman City of Sabratha lies 80 km (50 miles) west of the capital Tripoli. The port was established as a Phoenician trading post around 500 BC. It later became part of the short-lived Numidian Kingdom of Massinissa before being Romanised and rebuilt in the second and third centuries AD. The city was badly damaged by earthquakes during the fourth century, and was rebuilt on a more modest scale by Byzantine governors. Besides the well-preserved late third century theatre, that retains its three-storey architectural backdrop, Sabratha has temples dedicated to Liber Pater, Serapis, and Isis. There is a Christian basilica of the time of Justinian and remnants of some of the mosaic floors that enriched elite dwellings of Roman North Africa; the Villa Sileen near Al-Khoms is a good example. The mosaics are most clearly preserved in the colored patterns of the seaward (or Forum) baths, directly overlooking the shore, and in the black and white floors of the theatre baths. There is a museum adjacent to the site which contains some excavated artifacts, whilst others are displayed at the National Museum in Tripoli.

Leptis Magna is the largest Roman City in Libya, and its ruins are some of the most complete and best preserved in the Mediterranean. The city is arguably Libya's biggest tourist attraction. Leptis Magna was originally founded by the Phoenicians in the 10th Century BC. It survived the attention of Spartan colonists, became a Punic city and eventually part of the new Roman province of Africa around 23 BC. As a Roman city it prospered, with figures like Septimius Severus as one of its emperors. The city was sacked by a Berber tribe in 523 AD, and later abandoned and reclaimed by the desert. Although it provided a source of building materials to various looters throughout history, it was not excavated until the 1920s. Today the site has many monuments still intact. The theatre is the most obvious, and has good panoramic views of the city from its upper tiers. The Hadrianic Baths are another attraction, and one of the pools, measuring 28 times 15 meters, remains intact. This bathhouse was one of the largest that was ever built outside Rome. The circus, nearly a kilometer away from the main site, remains still only partly excavated. At 450 by 100 meters, it was one of the largest in the entire Roman world. It is also the only one of its kind in Libya today. The Leptis Magna Museum of Leptis Magna contains many excavated artifacts, as well as recent discoveries such as five colorful mosaics created during the 1st or 2nd century AD.

The Temple of Zeus in Cyrene, *Eastern Libya*
Although Cyrene was later incorporated into the Roman Empire, it was originally founded in 630 BC as a colony of the Greeks from the Greek island of Thera. 16 kilometers from Cyrene is the port of Apollonia (Marsa Sousa). The city promptly became the chief town of ancient Libya and established commercial relations with all the Greek cities, reaching the height of its prosperity under its own kings in the fifth century BC. Soon after 460 BC, it became a republic, and after the death of Alexander III of Macedon (323 BC) it was passed to the Ptolemaic dynasty.

Ophelas, the general who occupied the city in Ptolemy I's name, ruled the city almost independently until his death, when Ptolemy's son-in-law Magas received the governorship of the territory. In 276 BC Magas crowned himself king and declared de facto independence, marrying the daughter of the Seleucid king and forming with him an alliance in order to invade Egypt. The invasion was unsuccessful and in 250 BC, after Magas' death, the city was reabsorbed into Ptolemaic Egypt. Cyrenaica became part of the Ptolemaic empire controlled from Alexandria, and became Roman territory in 96 BC when Ptolemy Apion bequeathed Cirenaica to Rome. In 74 BC the territory was formally transformed into a Roman province.

The archeological site lies near the village of Shahhat. One of its more significant features is the temple of Apollo that was originally constructed in early 7th century BC. Other ancient structures include a temple to Demeter and a partially excavated temple to Zeus. There is a large necropolis approximately 16 km between Cyrene and its ancient port Apollonia. The Cyrene Museum also lies on the site.

Tripoli

Tripoli is the de facto capital of Libya and was once known as the "White Bride of the Mediterranean." Throughout history, the city exchanged hands many times, and several historic mosques and other sites in the medina attest to this. The Turkish and Italian colonial periods left a distinctive mark on the city's architecture.

Easily the most dominant feature of Tripoli is the Red Castle, Assaraya al-Hamra, which sits on the northern promontory overlooking what used to be the sea - a motorway and 500 m (1640 ft) of reclaimed land now separate the two. The large structure comprises a labyrinth of courtyards; alleyways and houses built up over the centuries with a total area of around 13,000 square meters (140,000 sq. ft). Inside, there is evidence of the entire city's (and thus the citadels) ruling parties: the Turks, Karamanlis, Spaniards, and Knights of Malta, Italians, and several others who all left their presence in its arts and architecture.

Martyr's square in the heart of Tripoli, where the Medina and the Italian quarter meet.

The entrance to the Jamahiriya Museum is on Martyr's Square, next to the castle. These facilities were built in consultation with UNESCO at enormous cost, and the exhibits within are laid out chronologically, starting with prehistory and ending up with the revolution. The most impressive parts are the mosaics, statues and artifacts from classical antiquity, which make up one of the best-preserved collections in the Mediterranean.

The Medina is the heart of Tripoli and provides the best sightseeing and shopping opportunities for tourists. The basic street plan of the medina was laid down in the Roman period when the walls were constructed as protection against attacks from the interior of Tripolitania, and are considered well planned, possibly better than modern street plans. In the 8th century a wall on the sea-facing side of the city was added.

Three gates provided access to the old town: Bab Zanata in the west, Bab Hawara in the southeast and Bab Al-Bahr in the north wall; the city walls are still standing today. The Bazaar is also known for its traditional ware; jewelry and clothes can be found in the local markets. Unlike neighboring countries, Libya is known for its lack of hassle in the souqs. The old walled city also contains virtually all of Tripoli's historic mosques, khans (inns), hammams, and houses. Other nearby attractions includes the city's zoo and many of the nearby beaches.

Since the rise in tourism and influx of foreign business people, there has been an increased demand for hotels in the city. To cater for these increased demands, the Corinthian Bab Africa hotel located in the central business district was constructed in 2003 and is the largest hotel in Libya. Other large hotels include the Bab El Bahr hotel and the Kabir Hotel as well as others.

Ubari Lake in the Sahara Desert.

The Sahara desert represents more than 90% of the Libyan territories and is an important Libyan resource with many tourist attractions. This includes historic arts, agricultural, urban constructions, and habitations in oases and desert lakes. Such diversity in desert tourist phenomena in Libya gives several opportunities to perform entertainment, cultural and scientific activities to satisfy the desire of the adventurer and the amateur sportsman tourists through the desert paths. Moreover, the natural beauty distinguishing the Libyan Desert and its calm, isolation and simplicity of life present unlimited photographic opportunities.

A Libyan dressed in traditional clothing in Ghadames.
The oases are considered in general among the most important desert tourist landmarks distinguished by their natural beauty. They are surrounded with sand dunes, and sometimes with

lakes. Some distinct landscapes add to the tourist attractions. This is in addition to the richness of the distinct oases, their cultural heritage, and unique styles. The most important oases in the area are Ghadames oasis, Ghat oasis, Wadi Elhayat oases, Wadi Eshati oases, Jufra oases, and Kufra oasis. They are the permanent rich green areas in the desert.

The Desert Mountains and hills in south Libya add other aesthetic aspects to the desert beauty.

Contemporary Travel

The most common form of public transport between cities is the bus, but many people travel by automobile. There are no railway services in Libya.

Libyan cuisine

Libyan cuisine is generally simple, and is very similar to Sahara cuisine. In many undeveloped areas and small towns, restaurants may be nonexistent, and food stores may be the only source to obtain your lunch.

Some common Libyan foods include couscous, bazeen, which is a type of unsweetened cake, and shurba, which is soup. Libyan restaurants may serve international cuisine, or may serve simpler fare such as lamb, chicken, vegetable stew, potatoes, and macaroni. Alcohol consumption is illegal in the entire country.

There are four main ingredients of traditional Libyan food: olives, olive oil, palm dates, grains and milk. Grains are roasted, ground, sieved, and used for making bread, cakes, soups, and bazeen. Dates are harvested, dried and can be eaten as they are, made into syrup or slightly fried and eaten with Bissau and milk. After eating, Libyans often drink black tea. This is normally repeated a second time (for the second glass of tea), and in the third round the tea is served with roasted peanuts or roasted almonds (mixed with tea in the same glass.)

Under former Prime ministers Shukri Ghanem and Baghdadi Mahmudi, Libya underwent a business boom, with initiatives to privatize many government-run industries. Many international oil companies returned to the country, including oil giants Shell and Exxon Mobil.

Tourism was on the rise, bringing increased demand for hotel accommodation and at Tripoli International. A multi-million dollar renovation of Libyan airports was approved in 2006 by the government to help meet such demands. Previously, 130,000 people visited the country annually; the Libyan government hoped to increase this figure to 10,000,000 tourists. Libya has long been a notoriously difficult country for Western tourists to visit due to stringent visa requirements. Since the overthrow of Muammar Gaddafi's government, there has been revived hope that an open society will encourage the return of tourists. Prior to the uprising, Saif al-Islam Gaddafi, the second-eldest son of Muammar Gaddafi, was involved in a green development project called the Green Mountain Sustainable Development Area, which sought to bring tourism to Cyrene and to preserve Greek ruins in the area.

SPECIAL PLACES TO SEE

The whole of North Africa, except Egypt, was known as Libya to the ancient Greeks and Romans.

"If you are looking for the crossroads of history and ancient empires Libya is the   place."

Sahara meets the Mediterranean here, and extraordinary Roman and Greek historical monuments overlaid with Byzantine splendor, attract tourists to its shores.

Sahara's picture perfect desert scenery, boasts of accessible and exceptional, palm-fringed lakes surrounded by sand dunes and it engulfs nearly 90% of Libya.

Extinct and bewitching volcanoes like **_Waw al Namus_** where black sand encircles multicolored lakes are awe inspiring and close by.

Libya has Egypt to its east, Algeria to its west, Chad to the south. It has open borders with Tunisia and Egypt, but its borders with Chad, Algeria, Sudan and Niger, are CLOSED TO NON-LIBYANS.

Following places are unique and worthy of a visit:

Tripoli

Tripolinians are blessed with the most beautiful picture perfect Mediterranean Ocean. It is difficult to take your eyes off from, the scores of varying greens blues and other bewitching color-waves of the ocean. Yet the edges of the beaches are full of rocks roughened by the slaphappy surf, beating on them day and night. Low tide sucking away the sand from under them and rattling and rolling them while the high tide smoothens and polishes them into artistically shaped pebbles of multiple Grey Brown and mixed magical color designs all over.

It has world-class museums, evocative Median, Italianate architecture, and the best restaurants in the country.

Leptis Magna

Unrivalled Roman ruins from one of the greatest cities in antiquity.

Sabratha

Splendid Roman City ruins. It had one of the finest theatres.

Nalut

An old town perched atop the Jebel Nafusa. These ruins boast of the fairy tale Berber architecture.

Al-Jaghbub

This is a remote desert oasis, in eastern Libya, where Saharan Palm trees and sand dunes encircle the Lakes. It is closer to Egypt and has under water reservoirs, and trees laden with sweet dates.

Tadrart Acacus

This is a desert area in western Libya and is part of the Sahara. It is situated close to the city of Ghat and not far from the Algerian border. "Tadrart" means 'Mountain.'

It has a particularly rich array of prehistoric rock art.

Jabal Acacus

It has one of the world's finest open-air galleries of pre-historic art. Stunning landscape and the home of the Tuareg.

Idehan Murzuq

Remote Sand Sea, this has a breathtaking landscape in motion.

Wadi Methkandoush

This has the desert's best open-air gallery of 12000-year old rock carvings.

Ghadames

It is the Enchanted Caravan town of the Sahara with wonderfully preserved traditional houses and labyrinthine of streets.

Cyrene

Here at the hilltop you see the ruins of the ancient Greece's most sophisticated and extravagant city.

TOBRUK

Here you come across poignant cemeteries, trenches, and iconic sites from WWII'S most resonant battlefields.

Tolmeita

This is the coastal city of ancient Greece with exceptional mosaics in its museum.

Jebel al –Uweinat

This depicts an isolated landscape of rare beauty with rocks and desert wildlife.

Qasr Libya

You will be amazed at the exquisite details of the magnificent Byzantine mosaics and their historical significance on visiting this site.

Ras Hilla

This is located in the Green Mountains (Jebel Akdar) zone, about 1300-km east of Tripoli.

We arrived high up in the mountains, driven in a Taxi, along hairpin-bent roads, with precipitous drops. Seeing a helicopter hundreds of feet below us made me feel a bit queasy.

The view was stunning but scary; the dazzling sea far below looked magnificent.

The Italians, before W.W.II built this nice road up top. The natural waterfall here is very popular with the Libyans.

On the drive downhill we fell in love with the beautiful bright mauve wild flowers (these looked like delicate colchicuns!)

179

On reaching Apolonian, we got out and spent couple of hours at this place of pre-Hellenistic settlement, consisting of Italian and Greek ruins.

About 12 km, east of here we came across caves, where the Libyan freedom fighters used to hide from the Italians rulers.

We saw a large bomb crater and behind a wicker fence, in one cave at Al Fadra, we saw fourteen newborn lambs. Italian fascist's plans for Libyan pacification was one of the cruelest and bloodiest in the history of European colonization. Our taxi driver was very emphatic when he told us, that the Italians murdered 50% of their entire population.

Hundreds of people were hung daily, but due to astute media control, there were hardly any witnesses. The world at large only learnt through the accounts of certain foreign media and the photographs sent by the Italian soldiers to their families, boasting and showing off their might!

The real honor goes to the resistance movement and their tremendous sacrifices. They gave their lives and fought to the bitter end. Little kids and women suffered the insensitive and brutal butchering by the Italians in the temporary concentration camps in the middle of nowhere, behind treacherous barbed wires.

PROPAGANDA CAN NEVER TELL THE TRUTH,

TRUTH CAN NEVER BE PROPAGATED.

****

FACTS ARE NOT FRIGHTENING.

TURNING YOUR BACK & RUNNING IS!

Krishnamurti

What is Change?

One form appears , and another disappears.

Can we say that the butterfly used to be a caterpillar?

A substance in the caterpillar takes on the form of the butterfly.

Swami Prajnanpad.

This leads me to the story of

Umar Mukhtar,

(A hero, a leader, and a fearless fighter for the freedom of his beloved country.)

Some of the Bedouin revolutionaries had been sucked into, the Colonial invasion. A few sold themselves for the cause of peace-at the cost of human subjugation.

The young Omar (Umar al Mukhtar) was 16 when his father passed away. He was brought up in his hometown under the care and tutelage of one of the Shuyookh, Hussein El Gariani (similar sounding name as Graziani, the Italian General).

He eventually developed a lifestyle of sleeping for 3 hours in order to get up in the last third of the night and recite Qur'an until fajr.

He memorized the Qur'an in its entirety and covered its recitals every week, irrespective of other hardships.

He set an example of his courage and wisdom for others to follow, as became evident from his caravan trails to Sudan as a young man. Most caravans bypassed the tracks where a notorious lion lived. He decided to face the crisis head on. While other members of his caravan were shivering with fear, he took a shotgun and went after the lion on his horseback. The lion was no match for, his venery skills, the tremendous speed of his steed and his super marksmanship. He brought back the lion's head to every one's surprise and veneration.

This earned him the name of *"Lion of Cyrenaica."* An upbringing of upright religiosity and daring tenacity had a massive effect on him. His character and volunteering spirit changed the course of not only his tribe but also the world of Muslims in the Post colonial Era. The old age of 73 did not stand in his way to fight the overwhelming might of the Italian war machine. His skills of guerrilla warfare, his super strength, heroic spirit, and superior zeal would put a well trained

Commander with all the modern machine guns and half his age to shame!
After a lapse of half a century as a teacher in a small school he was ready for action.
He was bitter and argued that their land had been forcibly and inhumanly taken away from them.
He proclaimed at the top of his voice that it was their God given right, to resist such injustice. He refused to be conquered. The new governor of Libya, General Rodolfo Graziani warned him that he would surpass his predecessor, who was recalled by Mussolini, since he had failed miserably in putting an end to Mukhtar's resistance. Little that he understood Omar's deep conviction, inspired by his religious beliefs to fight the Italian oppression.
It was his intense courage and willingness to die for what he believed in, that kept Mukhtar's resistance alive and flowing.

In October of 1911, Italian battleships reached the shores of Tripoli, Libya with intent to stay. The Italian's fleet leader "Farafelli" made a demand to the Turks to surrender Tripoli to the Italians or the city would be destroyed at once. The

Othman Turks fled and the Italians attacked Tripoli anyway, bombing the city for three days and thereafter proclaiming the Libyan population in Tripoli to be "committed and strongly bound to Italy." That would mark the beginning of a series of battles between the Italian occupiers and the Libyan Mujahedeen (the Arabic word for freedom fighters).

In 1912, in the city of Barga, Libya, Omar Mukhtar organized and strategized what would become the birth of the Libyan Resistance holy war against the invasion. A teacher by profession, Mukhtar was a master strategist in desert guerrilla tactics. He knew his country's geography well, and he knew how to use that to his advantage in his battles with the Italians who were not accustomed to desert warfare. Starting out with a only a few thousand men, he led his small mobile groups into skillful and successful battles with the Italians and then faded into the familiar terrain. Mukhtar's men attacked outposts, ambushed troops, and cut lines of supply and communication, leaving the Italians astonished and embarassed to be outsmarted and outmaneuvered by a "Bedouin,"Omar Mukhtar, who had coined his name in the history as an affectionate

"LION OF THE DESERT."

The Libyan resistance spread from the far western regions of the country (Zwara city) to the far east in the city of Salloum, and on down to the southern city of Fezzan. The Italians had the superior manpower and technology, but the Libyan mujahadeen had the kind of courage, and love for their county that any occupier would fear. Their numbers eventually grew from less than a thousand, at the beginning of the resistance, to six thousand. They united to protect and defend their land, freedom, and honor from the foreign invaders, and they fought as religious men, proclaiming the words Allahu Akbar (God is great) with every battle they encountered.

For the Italians, Libya was their "right" and they intended to make sure the Libyans understood that. Italy's deputy "Mazari", in 1914, stated "It's our obligation not to help in any way the Libyan nationalist, but to subdue and dominate them, and most importantly, to impose our presence on theirs, and to evict them to the Sahara."

In the mountainous region of Ghebel Akhdar ("Green Mountain") in 1924, Italian Governor Ernesto Bombelli created a counter-guerrilla force that inflicted a severe setback to rebel forces in 1925. Mukhtar then quickly modified his own tactics and was able to count on continued help from Egypt. Between 1927 and 1928, Mukhtar fully reorganized the Senusite forces, who were being hunted constantly by the Italians. Even General Teruzzi recognized Omar's qualities of "exceptional perseverance and strong will power."

Pietro Badoglio, governor of Libya from January 1929, after extensive negotiations concluded a compromise with Mukhtar (described by the Italians as his complete submission) similar to previous Italo-Senusite accords. At the end, Mukhtar denounced the compromise and reestablished a unity of actionamong Libyan forces, preparing himself for the ultimate confrontation with General Rodolfo Graziani, Italian military commander from March 1930.

Graziani, in full accord with Badoglio, Emilio De Bono (minister of the colonies), and Benito Mussolini, initiated another plan to break Cyrenian resistance, after the June offensive had failed. The hundred thousand population of Gebel would be moved to concentration camps on the coast and the Libyan-Egyptian border from the coast at Giarabub would be closed. Thus preventing any foreign help to the fighters and depriving them of support from the native population. These measures, which Graziani initiated early in 1931, took their toll on the Senusite resistance. The rebels were deprived of help and reinforcements, spied upon, hit by Italian aircraft, and pursued on the ground by the Italian forces aided by local informers and collaborators.

The Italian-Libyan war was a David and Goliath battle. The Italians had the numbers (tens of thousands of troops), the tanks, and war planes. The Libyans had old rusted rifles, their horses, and a tremendous courage and determination to liberate their country. In some battles, the ratio of Italian to Libyan was 1: 50-100. However, even with the technology and numbers on their side, the Italians knew they had something to worry. The courageous resistance of the Libyans lasted nearly 20 years, and resulted in great losses for the Italians. But even more damaging than the losses in artillery and the casualties, there was a loss in morale among the Italians. The Italians were embarrassed by the lack of power and control they had over the Libyan resistance.

In a desperate effort to weaken the resistance movement led by Mukhtar, the Italian fascists decided to imprison Libyan men, women and children in concentration camps. Entire tribes were imprisoned in desert areas hundreds of miles from their homes in mountainous regions. By holding these people in the camps, the Italians were weakening the Libyan resistance in two ways: they were cutting off economic and moral support for the resistance, and they were preventing more men from joining the resistance. Men and women were continually tortured, and the punishments became more severe whenever Mukhtar outsmarted the Italian army. About 125,000 Libyans were forced into these camps, about two thirds of which perished. One can only imagine the toll this must have taken on Omar Mukhtar. On the one hand he was fighting for the liberation of his country and people; on the other hand, with each of his successes, he was furthering their misery. Still Mukhtar was determined to continue the struggle.

General Rodolfo Graziani, described Mukhtar as:
"Of medium height, stout, with white hair, beard and mustache. Omar was endowed with a quick and lively intelligence; was knowledgeable in religious matters, and revealed an energetic and impetuous character, unselfish and uncompromising; ultimately, he remained very religious and poor, even though he had been one of the most important Senusist figures." Today Mukhtar is a the most respected Hero in Libya.

Mukhtar's struggle of nearly twenty years came to an end on September 11, 1931, when he was wounded in battle near Slonta, and captured by the Italian army.

The Libyan hero was treated like a prize catch by the Italian. Though now in his 70's, he was shackled with heavy chains from his waist and wrists because of the army's fear that he just might escape and continue the Libyan resistance. Mukhtar's capture was a serious blow to his people. He was given an unfair "trial" and sentenced to be hanged on September 16, 1931. When the sentence was read and Mukhtar was asked if he wanted to say anything, he replied, "From God we have come, and to God we must return." Mukhtar was hanged before his people (on orders of the Italian court) to ensure that the Libyan spirit of resistance would die with him. But Omar Mukhtar lived on in the hearts of his people, and remains a true symbol of defiance to oppression, not just among the Libyan people, but among all Arabs.

When asked if he wished to say any last words, Mukhtar replied with a Qur'anic phrase: "Inna lillahi WA inna ilayhi raji'UN." ("To God we belong and to Him we shall return."). On September 16, 1931, on the orders of the Italian court and with Italian hopes that Libyan resistance would die with him, Mukhtar was hanged before his followers in the concentration camp of Suluq at the age of 70 years.

Today, Mukhtar's face appears on the Libyan Ten-Dinar bills. His final years were depicted in the movie Lion of the Desert (1981), starring Anthony Quinn, Oliver Reed, and Irene Papas. In 2009, Libyan leader Muammar Gaddafi wore a photograph of Mukhtar hanging on his chest while on a state visit to Rome, and brought along Mukhtar's elderly son during the visit.

With the Libyan uprising beginning February 17, 2011, Omar Mukhtar again became a symbol for a united, free Libya and his picture is depicted on various flags and posters of the Free Libya movement. Rebel forces named one of their brigades after him.

Golf Courses

We passed the compound of Colonel Gaddafi residence on the way to our Hotel El Kabir. Concrete walls encircled this area by 20 feet tall security walls. The entrance was secured with barriers and 24 hrs Military guards. Above the walls I could see the upper floors of several apartment buildings where Colonel's personal guards lived. These buildings were well maintained compared to the drab, run down apartments I had seen elsewhere around the city.

I was told that Colonel Gaddafi lived in a tent in the center of the compound. He had several camels tethered nearby so he could have fresh camel milk whenever he wanted.

Next is a drive to Bin Ghashir Golf Course, some 60 acres of rolling sand with a few scrawny Eucalyptus trees. This second course was built in 1948/49. The Brits built the first course near Benghazi at the end of WW II.

The course had 18 small raised tee boxes, 9 dry (without irrigation and grass,) round flat sand greens, ill-defined fairways. The only maintenance was to smooth the sand between ball and cup before making the putt. A piece of synthetic grass was used to give a preferred lie for shots.

Mr. Gaddafi was interested in the concept of bringing tourists into the country. He appreciated the financial benefits available from tourism.

I again wondered where all the money from oil had gone. The Libyan people were living in bleak conditions, way behind most of those in Tunisia and behind many in Egypt.

Colonel was not seriously concerned about the wellfare of his citizens. He was a gardener who never watered his plants. He had no interest to develop brillient scientists, who could outsmart him!

There was another Golf Course which had to be budgeted for and built for the American and European senior staff and their families at Brega which was the task given to my department.

The task was to refurbish the old deplorable and dilapidated, 18-hole course.

The proverbial 19th hole (dry and with ZERO alcohol,) was to become a huge sized social club with almost all the modern amenities, relaxation facilities, Golf store, Restaurants and most modern attractions, but ABSOLUTELY no Alcoholic drinks.

The budget was being set for the full course and was estimated to be over 2 million dollars. It had to be executed in two parts, nine holes in each part.

It had to be built immediately to serve the present generation of foreign golfers. The speed of completion of this expensive project would depend upon the *actual* increase in the population of golf-loving western families. This again would have been based on the quality and sustentation of the political atmosphere and relationship with Gaddafi.

There are several predominant differences between this and a normal Golf Course known to most of us. For example the land there was full of dry sand, and the lot we had to work on was adjacent to the bewitching beauty of the Mediterranean Ocean. With the moon creating tidal waves which then resulted in frequent Gibblies (highest velocity sandstorms).

The sandblasting jet actions of the Gibblies required designing, several special counter measures, using materials to withstand the erosion caused by the Gibblis. We had to bring in highly experienced contractors to design and build structures upstream of the Golf Course. Also this course had no grass whatsoever. To accomplish several additional tasks, listed in the following paragraphs our budget was to be revised immediately and we obtained an additional two millions to start with. It was a go ahead at any cost!

To start with we built additional underground parking for the contractors, several trucks bringing in special raw materials and special compounds for the retaining walls. The Gibbli simply sandblasted windscreens, creating deep scratches and cracks.

The next phase was to rebuild all the fairways, Tee-off points, and the greens (I mean Browns) in the centers of which the holes had to be placed.

Without the slightest exaggerations I will tell you that fairways were not fair. They were full of eroded cracked hard soil, frequently studded with pebbles, exposed bedrock and haphazard cracks, under which the likes of rattlesnakes hide. The Tee-off points were manmade cakes of gravel, sand, and special retaining oils.

Petroleum products were used, to bind the loose desert soil, as they were available in abundance and free. Subsequently these were banned for safety reasons. It was costly, time consuming to get alternatives like Soybean oil, vegetable oil stocks. These were sought after because these were environmentally friendly and biodegradable. They penetrated below the surface and bond nicely with the bed materials. This way there were no toxic run off and the top surface formed a protective shield, without dissolution.

But in actual project for conserving time and capital we used crank oil. This was easy and as we rolled the surface it became as smooth as linoleum.

The whole site was dry (no grass anywhere.)

Tees and Greens performed much better when sand was mixed well with oil. We had laid down an impermeable cloth beneath the new Greens to protect the environment. This also kept the weeds from growing from below. By regular maintenance and re-oiling annually it retarded the growth of the grass/weeds population.

Sand runoff was also avoided during heavy downpours.

The construction of Greens started with a huge cake of oiled gravel 128ft in diameter, in several layers. Each layer was thoroughly leveled and compacted with heavy rollers, several times over.

After each height of one foot, the compacted surface was left to dry. Several dozens of porous drain tubes all around the area got rid of the underground moisture.

First I did not understand where the moisture could come from?

Later an old Bedouin man told me it is from the beautiful Mediterranean.

When they were thirsty they would turn-up big rocks carefully for desert snakes and to find water, underneath to drink. It was brackish in taste but we needed the salt to counter the deadly heat.

Finally when the mound was a meter high and hard, we compacted it several times.

We allowed a meter wide central lane 128-ft long to be kept as a wide diametric walkway.

This is entirely a one of a kind Greens. It is like a discovery. In the center of this lane, which was also the center of the Greens Circle we had the "Hole" in the dead center. Remember after all the compacting, the central walkway became much harder than the rest of the Greens. Your golf shoe spikes poked, as you traveled in it, to pick up the ball.

I hope I did not make it too complicated! Basically when you shoot a Birdie and it lands somewhere on the 128-ft area of the Greens. You then go to pick up the ball, stand at the exact spot, look towards the flag in the hole and walk in exact sized steps by the shortest distance to the central hole! Count accurately the numbers of full steps you had taken plus any partial steps. Now walk (THE REAL GREENS AREA),

194

counting the same numbers of steps plus partial steps, and put your ball down. This would roughly bring you the same distance away from the hole as in standard Greens, except that normally you would hit the ball from where it landed. But in this UNIQUE GOLF COURSE, you have to hit from approximately the same radius-distance! But here comes another peculiarity! The surface of the central track is not that smooth as you would normally expect in standard Greens –means Grassy Green!

Here the surface was wavy in both directions-it undulated on the length side as well as on the width side! In addition when you walked on it, your golf shoes would leave several holes in the path. So to give you a fare chance to pot the ball you have to run a very heavy iron roller, up and down! Even the ladies had to be able to do it.

The central bearing of this roller was always kept well lubricated.

As and when your ball eventually entered the hole, you celebrated all you want, but you also had to empty the hole taking away your ball and the heap of sand left behind. In addition you had to run that roller once again in that central diagonal Greens to wipe out the holes left behind by your golf shoes, the second time around.

The most troublesome part was the construction of the hole- that was used to retain the flag as well.

In actual practice with "Gibblies" – howling winds would fill up some holes, which were in the line of the dust storms.

The diametric pathway was kept fairly smooth by the use of a special two-sided rake. One side was toothed to create a grooved surface and the other side had a straight edge to create a smooth putting surface for the ball. Rake was dragged in a circular motion beginning at the hole and working away from it. Great care was taken not to expose the lip of the cup.

First we drilled a Hole 3 to 4 ½ inch diameter x 6 ft deep, in the dead center of the circular field!

Then we filled it with gravel to help with drainage.

Sand Green Cups consisted of two pieces, the sleeve in which the cup either slides in, or rests on the top of the sleeve, with a flanged rim. These cups were made of steel and had a hole in the bottom to allow for draining water.

The flag support was welded to the bottom. This enables the golfer to remove the stick, and drag the rake to smoothen the path, while cup stayed in the hole. The cup could then be removed to empty its contents.

These cups were cleverly designed with a central holder that could not only retain the flag but also take heavy knocks from the flag's flutter and swings with heavy blasts from the Gibblies. Every player, before and after each use kept the annular space around the flag clean from dust and dirt by the use of spray cans, consisting of special dissolvent fuels, to drain the sands. The top soil around these holes were specially slanted down, all around very smoothly, like a cone- shaped funnel

As explained earlier, each player was obliged to compact the diametric Green Strip twice during each encounter, using a heavy set roller. This was a smaller version for human use, and was a replica of the industrial size, used behind a huge tractor-trailer.

The layout and architecture of the sand traps was so attractive that when you stood at the Tee box they were really joyful to watch and visually stunning. Let us not talk about how the players used to hate them when they were challenged to wedge the ball out of the deep sand, and to bring them above ground, in a single smart sweeping swing. They also cursed when their eyes were filled with, the sand blown by the counter winds

▲ ▶ ▼ ◀

GUARD YOUR TONGUE,
FOR IT IS HIGHLY DANGEROUS
UNGUARDED WORDS
CAN CAUSE TERRIBLE DISTRESS.
A SINGLE BAD WORD CAN DESTROY
A VAST QUANTITY OF GOOD.
A WOUND CAUSED BY FIRE
WILL EVENTUALLY HEAL;
BUT A WOUND CAUSED BY THE
TONGUE LEAVES A SCAR THAT NEVER HEALS.

Valluvar

Appendix

(This Vicious World)

(Source: Appendix F of the Tartan History page)-Wikipadia. Showing that, slavery, mass graves, earth quakes, and Concentration Camps, etc. existed all over the world, through centuries. We list few examples below.

In Afghanistan, <1/2 million people, forced into slavery> between 1000BC to 1026 AD. 11,700 miles of road damaged & made unusable. The country has no railroads. Transportation route into Afghanistan is the Khyber Pass in Pakistan. 1990s: Drought, starvation, 70% unemployment, 400,000+ receiving charity wheat, fields dotted with landmines, while 3,400 tons of opium are produced. 2 million+ flee to Iran, 1 million to Pakistan, others to Tajikistan. Black sites are secret prisons in Afghanistan. People buried alive in the desert. One of 88 mass gravesites containing thousands of victims, was found in Cham Tala. Half a million people are homeless & there are 80,000+ homes reduced to rubble in Kabul.

In Albania: Shfaros Kamp [Extermination Camp]
Slavery, 1468 AD: Ottoman. Mass FamineBurreli [Concentration camp. Mussolini administered it from 1939 on], Vichy Camp de Concentration Mecheria [1942: 50 km South of Oran. Collection camp for prisoners of war]. Luanda [Portuguese-established capital city for slave trade. Forced labor used into the 20th century. Slave trade on Angola & the African coast, Free import of slaves & trade with black slaves or new Negroes from Africa, without charge at the unload.

In Argentina: Los desaparecidos forced people to disappear through assassination, and disposing bodies, where they will never be found.
Half the population was by then living on < $3 a day. Mass Graves in Eastern Roman Empire1991 Yerevan [Holocaust memorial for those slain during WWI: Armenian Genocide]. Red Cresent Concentration Camps Armenian Genocide. Inmates hanged or killed by morphine injection. Bodies thrown into the Black Sea, Ras Ul-Ain, and Bonzanti. Mamoura [1894-1896: 200,000+ dead. The starving Armenians became a cause celebre among European & U.S. humanitarians.

In Australia: Mass Graves. Sisters of the Good Shepherd Magdalene Asylums were involved in a major racket. His paper hinted at babies born in convents & girls in the laundries being killed off or dying from exhaustion & being buried in strange places – Alan Gill.
Broken Rites Australia, non-profit organization of survivors of church-related sexual, unhappily married woman who consulted a church pastor & was then sexually abused in the course of

198

counselling. They've also seen sick & medicated women abused by hospital chaplains. Within the Catholic Church, victims keep silent. Melbourne 's Victoria Market [child mass grave] Immigrant Detention center. Jails asylum seekers

Sutton Forest, Central Railway Station, Fantome Island Aboriginal Leprosarium [Prison near Ingham for Aborigines, Maori & Pacific Islanders. A 7 year old child was jailed for 10 years], Christian Brothers' Bindoon Orphanage [Possiblythe most appalling children's home ever to exist in Australia – Alan Gill, Orphans of the Empire, Slavery. Blackbirding refers to the recruitment of people through alleged trickery & kidnappings to work on plantations, particularly the sugar cane plantations of Queensland – Wikipedia. Lady Julianne: The Floating Brothel: 225 convict women of solid breeding stock, forced into sexual slavery. Ship journeys through the Carribean May 1789 to Sydney. One Scotswomen dies, 7 babies are born on arrival. Curtin [Wackenhut Correction's Immigrant detention center. Three year olds have been placed with their parents in punishment cells, teenagers sew lips together while on hunger strikes] Slavery was prevalent on plantations in Fiji & in Queensland.

Die Grabeln [Mass Graves mostly caused by Plague. 3000+ graves dating 1100 B.C. & more disturbingly, bodies of miners with implements buried near the old graves]. Nuremberg Trials: crimes against humanity. Iron curtain containing barbed wire & landmines. It was finally taken down with the Berlin Wall in 1989.

Investigations of local police forbidden by GeStaPo-Linz. <Hitler's birthplace. >

SS exhange uniforms with Luftwaffe & German Army POWs, escaping into the mountains of Austria & Bavaria in 1945. Todebadeaktionen: Bathing to Death: 3000. 4000+ gassed. Weber murder handicapped German & Austrian civilians with carbon-monoxyde. 32,000+ killed between 1942-1943]

St. Georgen [At St. Georgen. Gas chambers, crushed priests, lynching, starvation, cannibalism, shot, 600 beaten to death, 420 children between 4 & 7 / 1300+ adults exterminated with heart-injections by Josef Mengele. Red Cross Delegate Louis Haefliger asks Kosiek to prevent the murder of 25,000 Gusen inmates. The SS planned to blast all of them up with high-explosives in the KZ Gusen I & II tunnels along with the local population of St.Georgen & Gusen, to kill any potential witnesses at later trials]. KL Gusen III: Lungitz [At Lungitz. 1942: SS find a grave yard from the Bronze Age. Local population forced by US-troops to bury hundreds of corpses SS guards leave behind]. Buaynara [Plague]

Yucayos, a tribe of the Taíno, the first people Christopher Columbus encountered in 1492. He massacred, raped, and enslaved them.

In Bangladesh: Genocidal Famine

1770: Bengal Famine claims millions

199

1781: Opium produced under British Government monopoly & sold to China. 1857: Sepoy Mutiny: Indian Army vs England. 1858: Direct rule from England. 1905: Bengal State partitioned by Curzon, the Viceroy of India. Millions of Indians die in a famine. The huge tankers of wheat gifted by Argentina were dumped in the ocean. They never made to India. Curzon does nothing. 3+ million died, during the Great Bengal Famine in 1943. 1971: Biharis forced into squalid camps where they live to this day. Indo-Pakistani War resulted in 3 million+ dead & 10 million+ refugees fleeing to India. Textile Workers make 14 cents an hour.

In Antwerp Assembly camp. 28 convoys of 25,257 prisoners shipped from Malines to Auschwitz. Only 1,207 survived. Supersonic Rocket Jet Engine Flyer carrying 2,000-lb 3,709 VI & V2s bomb dropped on Antwerp, killing 4,239+, and wounding 6,362+, between Oct 7, 1944-Mar 30,1945

[Military fort on the Brussels to Antwerp highway. Jewish people's cards stamped Juif-Jood. Auffangslager: Waiting Camp received Jews & political prisoners before their transfer to Germany. Starvation, grass eating, tortures, hangings, shootings. People herded into wooden sheds. Before the Allies, came the last prisoners were death-marched to Vught.]

Ypres [WWI: Kindermörd: demolished by artillery bombs. poison gas]. Ardennes Offensive: Battle of the Bulge

In Belize [British Honduras]. 1638: colonized with slavery. Katranisanje [Mass Graves]

Maly Trostinec [1941: 500,000 killed. NAZIs tried to remove all traces of the camp. No survivors are known to exist].

Minsk [The Capital], Mir, Niesez, and Pinsk [SS Totenkopf: Death's Head divisions ride in on white horses looking for Jews & Bolsheviks. Igor Kravek recalls one cart with women tied up & another with their sons. 16,000+ killed. SS Officer Herman married Gretel Braun, sister of Eva Braun.], Ivanitchi [Village outside of Pinsk. SS Death's head tramples the victims with white horses. Nina Ijenkowa hears their screams & sees blood on the hooves. Vera Bulina says the people were forced to dig their own graves, shot, & dumped into them. One SS men played a mouth organ while others screamed at them to dance.

Slavery700 BC-1728 AD. Corporation of Plymouth: Guinea/Sierra Leone/Brazilian slave trade

Bight of Benin [Gulf of Guinea. Epicenter of the transatlantic slave trade. 15, 000 slaves per year or 5% of the population exported as part of the triangular trade].

Brong Ahafo [Slaves for West African gold mines, ivory, kola nuts, sorghum & wheat plantations, shea butter, ostritch feathers, cloth].

Dahomey [France invades, women raped by French soldiers. Palm oil plantations. Ga people starved to death.]

Ketu [Home of the Ewe people. Slavery in the Ghana goldmines & saltmines]

In Bhutan: Sanskrit for Highlands. -   Colonization

200

1600 -1700: Tibetan Lama ruler of religious & state affairs from Sikkim. England seizes

1865: Second Opium War (Arrow War) / Bhutanese Massacre: English kill.

1910 - 1959: British India takes control

1959: China claims Bhutan. 1980s Bhutanese political dissidents, civilians, Nepalese expelled or fled to Nepal, where they were admitted into united Nations-run camps. 1947-1959: Atomic testing. Inhabitants removed to Ujelang.

Peru wins independance from Spain. Upper half named after Simon Bolivar. He is president of Gran Columbia: Columbia, Venezuela, Panama, Ecuador, Peru, & Bolivia. More than half the people of all the Andean countries, with the exception of Chile, live below the poverty line.

Bosnia-Herzegovina Katranisanje [Mass Graves] 1992: UN Peacekeeping force. Herzeg-Bosna: Mostar, Sarajevo [Breadline Massacre. People deported to Jasenovac Death Camp.thousands of corpses, piled up], Medjugorje [Ustasha police mass grave in Bosnia-Hercegovina People thrown off of cliffs into the stone ravines below. Dynamite used to blow the dead apart] Iskoreniti [Extermination Camp]. Mass Graves.in Botswana.

Brazil: [Slave Refugee Camp]

1900: Bubonic Plague. 2003: Half the country's income goes to a tenth of its people. President Lulu da Silva pledged his top priority was ending hunger. Favelas: slums. Bahia State [children born to slaves would be free. 1888: Lei Áurea: Golden Law slavery abolished. 2003: More than half the sugar cane crop is cut mechanically, & more than half the country's cane cutters have lost their jobs. Debt slavery holds thousands of Brazilians prisoners on guarded ranches] Minas Gerais [1695: gold plundered & mined, financing Europe's Industrial Revolution], Copacabana [Incan City]

Rio de Janeiro: 1555: Sir Francis Drake, a slave trader in the Carribean, destroys 2.5 million Brazilian Tupi-Guarani & Tapuya. 1831: Caxias' police battalions. 1900: bubonic plague. Parana [NAZI Dr. Josef Mengele performs abortions without anesthesia]

São Paulo [1912: Rodon pacifies Kaingáng Indians. Nominated for a Nobel Peace Prize], Sveno Concentration Camp

Children from Burkina Faso & Mali migrate to the Ivory Coast, where these youngsters wind up as virtual slaves on the plantations]

W.W.II. - Environment of extreme social split: At the one extreme, the heaven of many well-paying jobs for the desirable haves; on the other, the hell of homelessness all the way to concentration camps for the undesirable have-nots' Wikipedia: Homelessness Population is starved to death.]

President Richard M. Nixon authorizes bombing of North Vietnamese bases in Cambodia; over the next four years dropping more than a half million tons of bombs on Cambodia. Estimated dead 600,000+. War Powers

Resolution: USA Congress refused to provide money for bombing beyond Aug. 15, 1973. Power to halt use of any U.S.armed forces the President has ordered into combat abroad. Ek [Killing Fields: Khmer Rouge closed schools, hospitals, factories, confiscating all private property & relocating people from urban areas to collective forced labor farms. Abolished banking, finance, currency, outlawing all religions. 3.3 million+ estimated dead. Buddhist stupa was filled with 5,000 skulls. Mass grave with 8,000 bodies], Tuol Sleng: Hill of Poisonous Trees [S-21 torture prison in Phnom Penh. Museum records state that of the 20,000 prisoners there only 7 have survived. Skull map of 300 bones dismantled in 2002. Leg irons. Executions by sharpened bamboo sticks, buried in mass graves. January 7, 1979 Vietnamese troops capture Phnom Penh, deposing the Khmer Rouge. Khmer Rouge retreat to the west, controlling an area near the Thai border for the next decade, setting off landmines & smuggling diamonds until 1999]

Canada: Iroquois for Villages

Slave Ships

Cillin: Mass Graves, for chilren. Saint John Co. Almshouse [children starved & made to work until dead]. 1846: William Craig raped Ann Payton. She bore his child. Found not guilty, received Irish famine emigrants who died of typhus & cholera from contaminated water. 1500-1884: Slavery. Belgian King Leopold II seizes Chad. Sara enslaved.

1990: Patriotic Salvation Movement

President Idriss Déby

Genocidio in Chile: Where the Land Ends

Santiago [1530: The Capital. Spanish expedition massacres, the Incas, Aymara, & Mapuche, 2700 BC: Emperor Huangdi & Emperess Xilingshi find white silkworm moths in the mulberry trees. Cocoons dropped in water unravel to silk. 500BC Confucius: Great master born. Disciples recorded his conversations & sayings in a book called The Analects. 256 BC - 202 B.C: Ch'in [Pure] Dynasty founder Qin Shih Huang Di builds the Great Wall.

Chinese is written in characters. There are seven dialects: Mandarin [Putonghua: Standard: Manchuria], Cantonese [Yue], Xiang [Hunan], Gan [Gan River, Jiangxi], Hakka [Guangdong], Min [Fujian], Wu [Shanghai]. Chinese is spoken with no tenses;Just vocabulary; No grammer.

1799: White Lotus Rebellion: Sichuan

1958-1962: Great Chinese Famine: Grain exported to towns & cities. 43+ million dead

1979: Pinyin System for writing Chinese in the Roman alphabet adopted by government

1997: Manchuria: Economic reforms. 25 million workers permanently lay off. 40% unemployment

Imperial Army invasion on Dec 13, 1937 looting & burning the area. US Navy gunboat Panay destroyed. 10,000 corpse ditch, 80,000+

women tortured, raped & killed. Surviving women forced into military prostitution. Babies speared to death with bayonets. Young men machine-gunned, decapitated, & their bodies dumped into the Yangtze: Long River. Chinese soldiers death-marched to Shanghai: 300,000 died.

April 2001 600 troops attack unarmed villagers, in Jiangsi Province. Farmers refused to pay high taxes. Payment had been demanded even in 1998, when floods destroyed the farmers' crops

Honan Province Villagers selling blood to get money to live on. Buddhism, urged people to live spontaneously, calmly accepting inevitable changes – even death.

1880-1910: Bubonic Plague. 1997: Hong Kong is now a Special Administrative Region of China, ending 156 years of British colonial rule. There are 180+ labor camps in China. Companies utilizing prison labor are exempt from income tax. 'China has a vast forced labor camp system & perhaps the most secretive & widely feared penal system in the world.' – Wu Hongda, Laogai Research Foundation

Xiguoyuan & Lanzhou Detention Centers inmates used to peel & crack melon seeds with teeth & bare hands in the frost. Blood & pus falling on the seeds marketed as Hand-picked Melon Seeds & exported to more than 30 countries including: the United States, Canada, Australia, France, New Zealand, & Southeast Asian countries. Those who do not meet their quotas are beaten to death.

Su Jinduo & Su Jinpeng, brother and sister, kidnapped at a Qingdao, Shanghai bus station during Chinese New Year, loaded onto a minibus with other children to a brick factory in the next province. Hundreds of children & adults have been kidnapped in Central China to work as slaves being fed only water and steamed buns. Parents have petitioned local authorities to crack down on the kilns, banded together to try to rescue their children. Local authorities have sometimes turned parents away from the factories in collusion with the kiln owners. Labor Inspectors have taken children from freshly closed kilns & resold them to other factories.

Guolaosi: Worked to Death

Bainan Toy Factory, Soonggang: 19-year-old Li Chunmei died after working a 16-hour shift at the Bainan Toy Factory in Soonggang. Guolaosi: over- work death applies to young workers who suddenly collapse and die after working exceedingly long hours, day after day. Local journalists say many of them are never documented but estimate that dozens die under such circumstances every year in the Pearl River

2007: Mattel's worldwide product recall of 19 million lead-paint toys. China's factories now produce nearly 80% of the world's toys. US Toy imports from China rose to 222 billion last year. 'Everyone tries to bribe the inspectors' Anita Chan Australian National Unversity – US toy importers share blame in recalls. Workers live in dormitories with up to 29 other workers per room. Slave labor forced overtime, no sick leave. McDonald's: Sewco Toy Factory

Spray painters supplied only a gauze mask. Workers operating dyeing machines lost half of their right palms & all of their fingers in accidents. 16-hour workday, after all charges & fees are deducted from the monthly wages, workers are left with nothing

Kwai Yong, Shenzhen [Heavy mesh covered the windows. Doors at the bottom of the factory's only stairway were locked to prevent workers making 7 cents an hour from leaving before they had met their daily quotas. After fire, when the last flame was doused, 87 workers were dead. Scores of others injured in 1993.]

KZ Lidice [Chelmo. 1942: SS unit kills all males: 172 of them Women seperated from their children and taken to Ravensbrück concentration camp. Town completely destroyed.

KZ Tremosna-Pilsen / Plzen [Pilsner beer from here. Severe abuse, death, dysentery, typhus, and dropsy. Bory Prison: Starvation related typhus]

Reinhard Tristan Eugen Heydrich & Hans Gunther receive Slavs & others racially unfit for Germanification. – Prague

Bypass built from Prague 60 km away to the camp. 50000+ per year processed at the Bohusovice railway station, starvation, typhoid fever, spotted fever, no sanitation. Death Marches. Autumn Transports: living witnesses, those, who knew too much, removed. 'The Terezin columbarium, filled with paper urns containing the ashes of prisoners tortured to death in Terezin & cremated in the crematorium of the camp, liquidated. About 17 thousand urns, possibly more, were dumped in the Ohe river, the remainder in a pit near the Litomerice concentration camp'. Denmark [Danuna: Water from Heaven]. Gravens [Mass Graves] Folkedrab [People Murder]

Dr Carl Vaernet: Human experiments on concentration camp prisoners. Pink Triangle Prisoners cured by synthetic hormone injections, lobotomies, & castration.

Vichy Camps de Concentration

1830 AD: Cholera kills 19,000

1855-1869: Suez Canal Company opens to shorten the route between England & India, concession to operate the canal until 1968

1948-1950: Arab-Israeli War: Palestine partitioned. Suez bans Israeli ships.

1956: Suez Crisis: Egyptian President Gamal A. Nasser seizes the canal & announces canal tolls will build the Aswan Dam. England, Israel, & France attack. 25,000 Mizrahi Jews expelled from Egypt. UN calls a cease-fire

1967-1975: Six Day War: Egypt closes the Straits of Tiran to shipping. Israel controls Gaza Strip & West Bank

1980: Anwar Sadat assassinated, current President Hosni Mubarak Gaza Strip [1998: Yasser Arafat & Binyamin Netanyahu share]

Northumbria Concentration Camps

1815: Corn Laws Sir Robert Peel prohibits the importation of corn until prices reach starvation level. Founder of the London Metropolitan Police Force named Bobbies after him.'Thousands die 40 or 50 deep in Liverpool's pestilent cellars. British merchant ships stuffed tight with quality foodstuffs arrive at Liverpool from Ireland throughout the famine years destined for the belly of the British bourgeoisie,' – Irish Holocaust

Assistance Institution: No baths, stone breaking, vagrant's cells, starvation on porridge & bread, Invasion of the Body Snatchers: Corporation of Plymouth. 1600: East India Company Inc, Messrs Worms of London Mortgage Bankplantations: sugar cane, lemon grass, citronella, indigo, coconut, cinnamon, tea, rubber & bananas.

Jamaican slaves, or the Triangular Trade in Indian workers. Joseph & James White: Baptist Mills Pottery: 1840 to 1891 Bristol Stoneware Glaze supplied to Doulton & Co, pipes. Closed down in 1891 due to slave labor conditions

Bethnall Green [1777: 1,400+. floors soaked with urine, no ventilation or water, and starved on suet pudding. There was the Mortuary, the Post-Mortem room, with revolving tables, and coffin lift. Infirmary located by graveyard with a surgical dissection room, dead house.

Whitechapel St Peter's Mint [1832: 600+ dead by starvation & cholera]

Kent: Clear Water, London: Greenwich Institution [1834: 1928+. Iron-gated Isolation hospital. Children segregated starved on bread & molasses, whipped, caned, & forced to serve rich food to the Board of Guardians. Boils, meningitis, typhus. Punishment for eating mulberries from the tree outside, weekend solitary confinement, children transported to Canada], Lesham [1612], Woolwich [I was student at the Woolwich Polytechnic; receiving scholarships; graduating from the University of London in 19 months, in june 1948 instead of the usual 4 ½ years].

Lambeth & Norwood [1726: 270+ weaving, stone-breaking, bathtubs filled with slime, watchtower, prison receiving block, isolation block for children under 8, crematorium].

Southwark- (1782): Mint St. Typhus, dysentery, and scarlet fever, open sewers. 1865, by the Thames River, people were seen boiling bones. 420 inmates inside, not having water for a week, starving on tea & bread, were forced to care for the dead. Average mortality was 300.

Surrey Industrial School [Gassed children to death], Parliamentary report listed parish workhouses in Battersea (I attended the special course at the Powerhouse in 1948.)

City of London: Central London: Highgate Mental Health Centre & Prison [1596: Consists of: Strand Workhouse, Highgate Cemetary & Archway Crematorium. Starving Women executed for trying to steal food, sexual   slavery/prostitution.

St. Pancreas [1788: 1900+ /yr. gangrene, smallpox. 1856: Florence Nightingale], Holborn(I visited, the Indian High Commission, several time in 1946-59.)-Orphanage & Prison
City of London: Homerton [1699: child labor, starved on bread & beer], Bow Road [1849: 800+ children died], London's Bridwell [1688: child labor. crematorium], Cotswald: bodysnatching, corpse theft & human dissection by London Company Surgeons. 7 pounds paid for each adult corpse; smalls or children paid by the foot & teeth paid by the piece to make dentures for the rich
Brookwood Cemetery: 1852: crematorium. Newgate Prisoners on trial; transported to Australia for prostitution, pawning & wheat theft], Newgate Prison [England's main criminal prison for 700+ years, torn down in 1902. Originally part of West Gate, entranceway to the city, rebuilt & renamed Newgate in the 1100s. Subterranian cells under the sewers. Rats, typhus. Children as young as 5], St. James Park [Borders St. James's Palace. Prostitution hub for rich men from West End], Trafalgar Square [Sunderland Inc. Crematorium]
East Anglia Concentration Camps [Headington Deathcamp's Infirmary]
Bardon [1765: used in Charles Dicken's Oliver Twist.Corpse Roads: The traditional medieval death-roads, or corpse-roads, ending at cemeteries, Guiltcross Home for Mental Defectives [1836: exercise yard, infirmary, inebriate reformatory. WWI: German POWs], Lihou [Connected to Guernsey at low tide by an ancient stone causeway. Vraic: seaweed harvested & dried on frames set up on the beach. 1927 factory produced iodine from seaweed. All traces of the industry disappeared during the German Occupation], Ethiopians impaled, black shirts of the fascist Militias kill all of the men, women & children they encounter in the streets. Homes in flames, mass executions of groups of 50-100 people], Oromio [Oromo people of Oromia massacred by Mililik I with European powers & land seized. Survivors sold as slaves, children, & elderly burned alive.] 1935: Mussolini proclaims the Empire of Italian East Africa. Mustard gas grenade bombs dropped from airplanes, phosgenes sprayed like an insecticide on villages. Gas, flamethrowers. Forced labor camps, public gallows, mutilated corpses. Italian troops photographed next to cadavers hanging from the gallows or hanging around chests full of decapitated heads. 1974: the Dergue depose Emperor Ras Tafari Makonnen Haile Selassie, who had ruled since 1928. Afterwards are bloody coups, uprisings, taxation, and wide-scale drought, People dislocated & herded into socialist villages. Millions starve to death while agricultural products: coffee, pulses, hides, skins, oilseeds are exported to the U.S., Germany, & Japan. Millions flee as refugees. Ethiopia becomes a Communist state in 1984, with Mengistu as secretary-general of the newly established Workers party. Dergue replaced by Tigrayan & Eritrean guerilla armies in 1991. Eritrea declared independent in 1993. The Ethiopian People's Revolutionary Democratic Front has incarcerated tens of thousands in concentration camps. [Work Camp], Koveri [Work Camp]

Sexual Slavery Immigration law allows the state to deport immigrants suspected of prostitution without a trial; thus in cases of physical abuse by the pimps, the prostitutes cannot even resort to the police. – Wikipedia

Les Cryptes [Mass Graves]

Génocide [People Killing]

La Crypte: Paris Catacombs Underneath the Gare Montparnasse TGV station. 6 million body parts. Le Cimetière des Innocents Green Man stalks & eats vagrants. Little Devil of the Quarries has bleeding eyes, wild hair. Galleria de Paris [graveyard exhumed in 1789], Père-Lachaise Cimetière [monuments to the Holocaust], Montfaucon [hanged & left to rot until their bones fell. grave pit], Le Cimitière de Saint Hilaire, Marville [sculptured gravestones. An ossuary stacks 40,000 skulls: some enclosed in a wooden case], Nantes [For miles round the country was bare, for the enemy had cut down every tree & burnt every blade of corn; inside the gates men were dying of famine. During the 18th century, Nantes was the slave trade capital of France. Reign of Terror: Thousands of summary executions by drowning in the Loire river. Bombed twice in WWII], L'église de Kernascleden and several other locations suffered from widespread plague. Mass-graves, corpses lie scattered around city. Marseille's 90,000 dead. 50,000+ die as plague spreads north to Aix-en-Provence, and other neigborhoods.

Frontstalag / Bastilles [Prisons] Torture.

Oscar Méténier set up the theatre in the Paris Montmartre red-light district specializing in torture plays. It did not close down until 1962. The largest prison in France, built by architect Henri Poussin in 1895. Used as a torture chamber during WWII. Dark holes, mass execution by the GeStaPo. Camp de concentration Victiu Vichy: Internees, young children starved to death, exposed to extreme cold. Camp filled with vermin & mice. 1957: 14,000+ Algerians interned Promotion paysanne writes the French Minister of Agriculture & engages in civil disobedience. They have nothing left to lose. The letter documents starving farmers deprived of their livelihood comitting suicide]

The mountains border Germany, Belgium, Luxembourg, & Switzerland. 45,000+ dead, exécution crématoire ashes thrown in garden, gas chambers, electrocution, whipped to death, phénol injection NN: Nacht und Nebel: Night & Fog members of resistance movements in France, Belgium, Russia, the Netherlands & Norway. Coded 14 on punch cards. Human experiments without anaesthetic, vivisection, stérilisation, dissection mustard gas, typhus, epidemic jaundice at l'Institut d'Anatomie de Strasbourg. Professeur Hirth said the 86 corpses he had were only sleeping & used his Swiss passport to return to Germany. Westwald [These children are later called Cursed Children & their mothers]

Lambarene [1912: Hospital built by missionary Albert Schweitzer (1875-1965) of Strasbourg, Nobel Peace Prize Winnings used to build a leper colony]. UN War crimes included Forced Maternity & Sexual Violence. 1933: All abortions outlawed & doctors who violate the law executed. Women are removed from the work force & encouraged to have children, whether they are married or not. Nazis promote Aryan births through marriage loans, child subsidies & official decorations for hero mothers of four children or more. 1936: SS Maternity Homes established by Heinrich Himmler for racially pure women & girls to give birth in secret. Children adopted by the NAZI party. Himmler offers promotions to SS Men based on the number of offspring they produce. Kidnappings, Germanisation & subsequent killings of thousands of children from the occupied countries, continued.

20,000 German slave labor camps existed.

Barth [Dorothea Binz, La Binz, head training overseer at Ravensbrück after 1942, trained her female students, numbering 1000, on the finer points of malicious pleasure. One survivor at the camp stated after the war that the Germans brought a group of fifty women to the camp to undergo training. The women were then separated & brought before the inmates. Each woman was then told to beat a prisoner. Of the fifty women, only three had asked for a reason & one had refused. The latter was subsequently imprisoned. Binz supervised mass shootings, killings in the gas chambers, mass deaths by starvation, neglect, severe abuse, & cold. She reportedly carried a whip in hand along with a leashed German Shepherd & at a moment's notice would kick a woman to death or select her to be killed. She also hacked people to death with an axe. Ruth Closius-Neudeck, Blockführerin: Barrack Leader famous for cutting the throats of inmates with the sharp edge of a shovel, promoted to head of the Barth camp in 1944.]

1972: Kurt Waldheim, former member of the Waffen SS & responsible for the mass genocide of Jews, Slavs, Greeks, & Gypsys in the Balkans, is elected Secretary to the United Nations, exports UNDOF: United Nations Disengagement Observer Force forces to Syria, Israel & Egypt & becomes president of Austria in 1986. When he becomes knighted from the Vatican, the Serbs block a visit from the pope.

Athens [Site of the plague in 430 BC with 1000 tombs. The plague killed 1/3 of the populationn. WWII: The center of NAZI administration & a work camp. The administration starves the civilian population.], Arcadia, Salonika [Work camp], Thrace [80 percent of Jewish residents murdered],

1966: About half of Guyana's people are East Indians whose ancestors were brought from India to work on plantations. About 40 percent Guyana's people are black whose ancestors were brought from Africa as slaves.

Ardnamona [Board of Education evicted & starved people], Castle Fleming [17 yd plot has head-stones, marking the graves of unbaptized children], Galway Workhouse [1839-1921:

1000+ inmates. Newcastle Rd., Killeen: infant's graveyard on site], Ballykilcline [Co. Galway. Population of 8000 evicted & starved. Mass graves].

Accounts of the roots of Los Penitentes date back at least a thousand years to the flagellant orders in Spain & Italy. ... These men whip themselves with a short whip: disciplina during Holy Week, carry heavy crosses: Maderos, & tie their limbs to crosses to hinder the circulation of blood on Good Friday. A wooden wagon, el carro de la muerte: the cart of death bore a figure representing death & pointing forward an arrow with stretched bow. This procession went through the streets to the church, where the Penitentes prayed, continued their scourgings, returned in procession to the house: morada. Similar to the Muslim festival where they beat their chests with chains.

Chapel ruins with a Reilg: ancient graveyard. Tombstones in Irish], Lismore Workhouse [1744: In Líos Mor. Sir Richard Musgrave constructs mass grave with forty bodies dumped per week: Cork Examiner: 3 May 1847. 700+ inmates per year with two mortuaries, one across the road from the railway station & the other next door to the childrens' schoolroom. Duke of Devonshire employs inmates on drainage], Waterford Workhouse [Port of Waterford on the River Suir. 1785. 13% inmates killed in 10 years on gruel. fever hospital added 1799. cupping machine purchased to draw blood in 1848. records of people admitted destroyed. Soup out of boiled bones, open cesspit. People gassed, buried at St Otteran's. Shandon House is a Waterford cholera grave near Dungarvan], Waterford Magdalene Convent Laundry. Captain Wynne, the District Inspector for Clare, Christmas Eve, 1846: There is no doubt that the Famine advances upon us with giant strides. The effects of the Famine are discernible everywhere; not a domestic animal to be seen. It is an alarming fact that, this day, in the town of Ennis, there was not a loaf of bread ...I ventured through the parishes to ascertain the condition of the inhabitants. I witnessed, more especially the women & little children, crowds of whom were to be seen scattered over the turnip fields, like a flock of famished crows, devouring the raw turnips, mothers half naked, shivering in the snow & sleet, uttering exclamations of despair whilst their children were screaming with hunger. I am a match for anything else I may meet here but this I cannot stand. I have traversed a considerable extent of my district this week & I find distress everywhere on the increase. Without food we cannot last many days longer; the Public Works must fail in keeping the population alive. The workhouse is full, & police are stationed at the doors to keep the numerous applicants out; therefore no relief can be expected from that quarter.

Co Dublin [Black Pool]: Balrothery [1841: Union Workhouse 3 miles NW of Lusk. Held Belgian refugees during WWI], High Park Convent Laundry [Drumcondra, County Dublin. Run by the Sisters of Our Lady of Charity. 1993: The Remains of 155 inmates, who had been buried in unmarked graves on the Sisters of

Charity RTÉ interviewed Ms Kathy O'Beirne (45) who was repeatedly raped there between the ages of 12-14 & became pregnant. The Sisters deny she or any other pregnant girls ever worked there or that babies were born. The babies were found buried in the back of the laundry in 2003. Nuns May Sue RTÉ Over Sex Abuse Claim on Radio Show Irish Independent, August 4th, 2005], Rath Domhnaigh: Ballabuggy [1880: walled-in by Board of Guardians. the headstones are all rude & uninscribed. The Moat ancient desecrated graveyard. Human skulls, & bones. South Dublin: Foundling Hospital & Workhouse of the City of Dublin-Trinity College-St. James Hospital [1702-1916: 160 people sleep in bunk-like beds crammed into the workhouse cellars 240 ft long x 17 ft wide. Beggars, disorderly women, old, infirm, orphans diet of bread, milk, porridge, gruel, & burgoo: oatmeal in cold water seasoned with salt & pepper. At one of its gates, a basket was fixed to a revolving door. Someone wishing to leave a child anonymously could place it there, ring the porter's bell, & then depart. Infanticide: 1702: 260+, 1757: 700+, 1790-1796: 12,786 admitted. 5,216 dead in infirmary, 1797-1826: 52,150 admitted. Out of which, 41,524 were dead. 1797: Irish House of Commons reports children stripped naked at the infirmary, laid in groups of five & six crushed together in cradles, swarming with vermin, covered with filthy, dirty blankets cast as unfit for use. The Hospital nurse then gave them the Bottle, which the Surgeon claimed, helps them to die].

The Vatican has its own mail system, railroad stop for freight, telephone, water supply, lights, street-cleaning, bank, radio broadcasting tower, printing plant & jail.

Jamaica: Spanish for Hibiscus

Slavery

1519: Spanish governor of Jamaica sends Alonso Alvarez de Pineda to explore the Gulf Coast from Florida to Mexico.

1660: Charles II of England seizes, starts the Royal African Slave Company. A reward is offered for Juan de Serras, leader of one of the free settlements

1737: Maroon Wars: Windwood Maroons led by Nanny, the African Queen. Leeward Maroons lead by Cudjoe. They free slaves in Jamaica. Nanny makes a vow on Pumpkin Hill in 1737 to fight the British to the death. When she signs the treaty she is wearing their dead teethSaint James [1830: Emancipation Rebellion of Western Jamaica: Sam Sharpe & 20,000 slaves set the Kensington sugar works Estate in St. James on fire. 201 rebels killed in fighting the combined forces of the British army, navy & local militia.]

Japan [Nippon: nitsu: sun + phon rising / Zipangu: Marco Polo: Land of Gold]

James Franck (1882 -1964) Kaiser Wilhelm Institute, Nobel Prize jointly with Gustave Herz at Göttingen Physics Institute for electron theory. 1933: Atomic reactor University of Chicago Franck report 1945: 7 scientists issue warning.

Edward Teller: Physicist at Goettingen,   helped in the development of the H-bomb

Leo Szilard: Kaiser Wilhelm Institute fathers of the atomic bomb.

Max Born: (1882-1970) Göttingen Institute of Theoretical Physics Director, 1954: Nobel Prize for quantum mechanics at Edinburgh University

Werner Heisenberg: 1932: Nobel Prize University of Leipzig Atomic Physics. 1941-1945: Kaiser Wilhelm Institute of Physics Director

Hiroshima [Nobel Prize winner Albert Einstein Kaiser Wilhelm Institute of Physics. Nazis put 50,000 Reichsmarks on his head & he warns that Germany might acquire sufficient quantities of uranium to produce extremely powerful bombs of a new type The Atomic bomb dropped on Hiroshima by Lt. Col. Paul Tibbetson from the B-29 superfortress Enola Gay]. Nagasaki: Long Peninsula [In the Kyushu region. Setting for Giacomo Pucchini's 1904 opera byMadama Butterfly. An Atomic bomb dropped by Major Charles W. Sweeney from the B-29 superfortress Bockscar exploding 1,540 feet above the ground. There were no survivors within a 500-yard radius, of Ground Zero, the points above, which the bombs exploded. People outside that lethal range saw a brilliant blue in the first seconds. – Subsequently they noticed a white flash that became a burgeoning orange ball, emitting unbearable heat. Almost at once a violent blast of air shredded buildings, clothes & flesh, & everything combustible seemed to take fire]

May 1946, after the war, Einstein, presiding over the National Commission of Nuclear Scientists, declared: 'The release of atom power has changed everything except our way of thinking, & thus we are being driven unarmed towards a catastrophe... The solution of this problem lies in the heart of humankind.'

Tokyo Shokonsha: [The shrine has performed Shinto rites to house the kami (spirits) of all Japanese and former colonial soldiers who have died in conflicts. Formosan Taiwanese who arrived to request the removal of their relatives from the shrine and to perform spirit-calling ritual prayer for the return of their ancestors' souls were denied entrance, met by protesters & police. Tokyo also bombed on April 18, 1942, in the Doolittle Raid by the USA.]

Iwo Jima Island [21,000+ Japanese troops bombarded by aircraft. 25,000 marines, 30 per cent of the landing force, killed or wounded.

Okinawa Island [April 1, 1945: Allied troops pour ashore. Japan sends kamikazes to attack the landing force. Battle ends June 21, kamikazes sunk 30+ ships, damaged 350 others, 50,000 casualties. 110,000+ Japanese died, including many civilians who chose to commit suicide rather than be conquered.]

Aerial bombing during World War II rained destruction on civilian as well as military targets. Many cities lay in ruins by the end of the war, especially in Germany & Japan. Land battles spread destruction over vast areas. After the war, millions of starving & homeless people wandered among the ruins of Europe & Asia. In addition, millions of people died in fires, of diseases, & of other causes after such essential services as fire fighting & health care broke down in war-torn areas.

Enjo Küsai [Child Prostitution]

Enjo küsai, compensated dating, is a practice in Japan where high school-aged girls are paid by older men to accompany them on dates and / or to render sexual services? 5 to 13 percent of high school girls engage in enjo küsai. Telephone clubs supply customers with a list of mobile numbers.

Occupied by England after WWI

1946: Palestine partitioned into Israel, Jordan, West Bank, and Gaza Strip. 1948: Independence. 1353-1828: Lan Xhang Kingdom seized by Siam 1885: Union Indochinoise: French Indochina with Vietnam & Cambodia

In Laos, canoes traditionally opened a path through the water of the Mekong so those mythical serpents could come forth & bring rain to the rice fields.

Kara noziegumi [People Murder]

1715: Great Northern War: Prussia, Russia & Denmark vs Sweden over control of Estonia, Livonia, Karelia [Finland] & Baltic Waterways. Frederick I Wettin of Prussia wins Livonia, orders all Gypsies over 18 years of age to be hanged & hunted for sport through 1835. 100,000+ dead, 100,000 handicapped by injuries, during 15-year war. Civil War]

Lesotho Mass Death Liberia Mass Graves

Rise in the cost of rice causes riots & looting. Starving people, were eating snails, leaves & flowers bulbs boiled for three hours. Warehouses of the port stocked with foodnational suicide. Starvation, Dead bodies, often mutilated, dumped on the streets of the city or washed up beaches. Bodies not picked up because people fear being labeled as rebels.]

In Libya [Tripoli / Italian North Africa]

Campos de Concentracion

December 24, 1951: UN grants independence

1969: Muammar Muhammad al-Qadhafi's military revolt overthrows the ruling monarchy Tripoli /Tripolitania / Beida [Seaport. Originally a Roman Province then ruled by the Ottoman Empire until seized by Italy in 1912. US Embassy sacked in 1979. US Bombing raid in 1986 kills 60. Accused of Human Rights abuses. Moammar al-Qadhafi], Cyrenaica [600 BC Greek Province. 1942: England seizes], Fezzan [SW Province. 1942: France seizes]

Lithuania, Ypatingi Buriai [Death Squads]

Ponary [Jacob Gens' Einsatzkommando 9, assisted by Ypatingi Buriai: Special ones kill 5000 Jewish men, another 47,500. 80 prisoners kept to open up the mass graves & burn the bodies].

Telsiai Prison [Punishment squad led by

Donrsov called to liquidate prisoners in 1941 in Rainai Woods. 80+ tortured, mutilated & killed. The Soviets cut off tongues, ears, genitals, scalps, put genitals into mouths, picked out eyes, pulled off fingernails, made belts of victims' skins to tie their hands, burned them with torches & acid, crushed bones & skulls, & was done to living Vilnius [Capital of Lithuania. European Volunteer Movement WWII] Liquidated 3700 sent to camps in Estonia & Latvia; 4000+ children, women, old men sent to Sobibór. 1000+ went into hiding in the Rudninkai & Naroch forests.

1918: NAZI Josep Tito Broz declares himself president of Yugoslavia. Gostivar, Tetovo, Struga, [Invaded by the Albanian SS] Bulgaria rounded up more than 7,000 Yugoslavia/Macedonian Jews & turned them over to Germans, who deported them to the death camp at Treblinka in March 1943.

Malawi: Land of Flaming Waters -Slavery

Malaysia [Malacca / British Malaya / British East Indies]. Slavery

British Borneo Company / Royal Dutch Shell

Bahasa Melayu: Malay language from Sumatra.

1824: Anglo-Dutch Treaty divides British Malaya & Netherlands East Indies: Indonesia.

1930s Depression

1948-1960: Batang Kali Massacre-Malayan Emergency: Workers fight plantation owners. Special Air Service Jungle commando unit, Special Constabulatory Unit, Gurkha Unit. 1950-1952: Transmigration Programme-Resettlement Plan: Resettlement of half a million plantation workers into 500 Resettlement Camps with round-the-clock armed sentries & barbed wire fences. Military police inspecting identity cards. Which are used for rice rationing Tin, timber, resin, petroleum, gold mines insured by Lloyd's of London. English plantations: tapioca, gambier, spice, cocoa, bananas, pepper, coffee, Ulu Tilam Rubber Estate, palm oil have indentured servants from India, southern China. 1822: Sir Stamford Raffles (there is a famous Hotel in Singapore, with the same name), & Lieutenant Philip Jackson colonizes Singapore by segregating people into four areas. European Town: European traders, Eurasians, & rich Asians. Chinese Kampong: Chinese, Chulia Kampong: Indians, Kampong Glam: Muslims, Malays, Arabs. 1963: British Malaya becomes Malaysia with acquisition of the British territories North Borneo, Singapore: Lion City. Affirmative action creates a discontented class of educated but underemployed Malays. Chinese-majority Singapore seceeeds in 1965. 1969: Race riots, emergency rule & a curtailment of political life & civil liberties which has never been reversed 1999: Unisys Smart Card introduced. 2006: Amnesty International has criticised Singapore for having possibly the highest execution rate in the world per capita. British Gurkha regiment is the Singapore Police Force. Mandarinization Program: The decision of the government to dub Hong Kong Cantonese

& Taiwan Min programs into Mandarin when 16% of the Chinese population actually speak Cantonese, 65% speak Min & the rest speak Southern Chinese dialects not related to Mandarin. – Wikipedia.

Prostitution: In Medan, North Sumatra [Prostitution and syndicate trafficking of Indonesian girls & women from Medan to Malaysia. Syndicate makes identity cards & is accused of working with immigration officials to facilitate the departure of the women. Junior high school graduates told they will have good jobs as cellular phone shop attendants & then forced into prostitution. – Jakarta Post]

Mali: Hippopotamus [French Sudan] Mass Graves.

1550 AD: Peruvian Inquisition: Inca Empire that extends from Panama to Chile demolished under Spanish King Phillip II & Queen Mary I Bloody Mary of England. 30+ million killed, only 1.3 million remain.

Moche people: pyramids

1700: Bogotá becomes the capital city of The Viceroyalty of New Granada which contained the areas that are now: Colombia, Venezuela, Ecuador, Peru, Bolivia, & Panama.

18th Century: Great Rebellion in the Andes: Under Tupac Amaru II

In Phillipines: Spanish King Phillip.

1824: Independence –Genocidió.

1898: Spanish-American War USA seizes. US Military Governor: Elwell Stephen Otis

1900: US Military Governor: Arthur MacArthur III. 1901: William Howard Taft sets up colonial government. Aguinaldo captured.

WWII: Japan vs USA. 1946: Independance

1949-1954: Huks want land for poor farmers.

1965-1987: Ferdinand Marcos: Martial Law: 1972-1981; 1986: Marcos wins election against Widow Corazon Aquino. Roman Catholic Bishops hint at election fraud

1987: Marcos, family & some supporters airlifted out of the Philippines by U.S. Air Force after mass demonstrations.

1989: Marcos dies, believed to have stolen millions.

Luzon Island [1898: Battle of Manila: 1899: Manila Slaughter: 3,000+ corpses line the streets. 1900. 15 Filipinos killed for every one wounded. 1902: Batanga Province burned by General J. Franklin Bell, Areas outside the concentration camps called dead zones. 1941-1944: WWII Japanese troops vs Generals Douglas MacArthur & Wainwright. Naval base], Bataan Peninsula [1941: Bataan Death March: General Douglas MacArthur withdraws malnutritioned-diseased troops. 75,000 troops surrender to the Japanese, forced to march 65 miles to prison camps], Corregidor Island [Some US Troops survived until May 6, 1941. By then the Japanese were victorious everywhere.], Mindoro [Northern

Island. coconuts, rice, mahogany], Mactan [April 27, 1521 Ferdinand Magellan killed by islanders. Ship Concepcion abandoned], Palawan, Visayan Islands [7000 islands: Samar: 1901: Balangiga Massacre: In retaliation for an attack on Company C led by Thomas Connell & Lt E.C. Bumpus, USA Brigadier General Jacob Hurd Smith orders all Filiipinos over the age of 10 to be shot dead on site. Littleton Waller burns 255 villages in 11 days

In Poland: Plain in Slavic. In the town of Sztutowo 34 km from Gdansk city: Crematorium & gas chambers expanded in 1943 for Endlösung: The Final Solution Estimated dead 85,000+. Herta Bothe concentration camp guard who death marched prisoners to Bergen-Belsen in 1945. Prisoners murdered using phenol injections to the heart. Museum has the utensils, surgical bed, & needles. A ring of symbolic stones marks the holocaust stake. A 500 metre walks through the forest, to an excavated mass grave. Jews executed by firing squads, their bodies then burnt on funeral pyres1945: Baltic Sea mass grave for drowned people on torpedoed refugee ships, sinking of the Wilhelm Gustloff remains the worst maritime disaster of all time, killing 9,000+ people. 2005: Russian scientists found over 5,000 airplane wrecks, sunken warships lying in the bottom of the sea.

Stutthof SK-III: In Graudenz / Grudziadz SS Aufseherin Jenny Wanda Barkmann, Beautiful Specter, tortured people to death, selected women & children for the gas chambers. Arrested in May 1945 while trying to leave a train station in Gdansk. At the Stutthof Trial she is said to have flirted with her prison guards & was apparently seen arranging her hair while hearing testimony. She was publicly hanged on July 4, 1946, on Biskupia Gorka Hill near Gdansk

KZ Kolkau Female Concentration Camp

Commander Ewa Paradies arrested by Polish officers in Lauenburg, May 1945 At the Stutthof trial, several witnesses told of Paradies abuse. One told the court, 'She forced a group of women prisoners, in the dead of winter to undress. Then she poured icy water over them. If they moved then she would beat them.' Paradies was found guilty of murder, hanged on Biskupia Gorka Hill near Gdansk

Außlager: Satellite Camps: Bromberg / Bydgoszcz [30 km away. 85,000+ dead, 200 gassed in one month

Hermine Braunsteiner

Leopold Göth featured in Schindler's List. SS-Sturmbannführer Willi Haase orders a list of 4000 ghetto inmates for deportation. 7000 Jews deported, 600 shot, home for the aged & orphanage liquidated. Göth executed 2000+ people alone from the ghetto in one day. Göth shut down the concentration camp ordering the inmates to be murdered on the spot. Stole many millions of zloties worth of valuables], KZ Tarnow [Göth killed an unknown number of people on the spot. Others died through asphyxiation during transport by rail or were exterminated in other camps, in particular at   Auschwitz.]

Varsovie [Ghetto liquidated. Camp installed on the ruins].

Radzillow [1942: 3000 Revolt. 1,500 killed. 1,500 escape to in the forests, Another 3.500+ mass murdered in Palmiry, Warsaw, Firlej. Alfred Lipson "A few days later a young man came back. He had found a hiding place after the train stopped at Treblinka. He hid under the train by the wheels. He grabbed my coat by the lapels & with a frightened look in his eyes he said, I was there, I was there. They were all gassed. I wouldn't listen. NAZIs seperating people into two groups, shooting the unemployed. Survivors forced to dig a grave & dump the corpse in. "There were five hundred, maybe six hundred, laid out like herring".]

Polen-Jugenverwahrlag [Polish Children Camp]

Poland's second largest city walled off by barbed wire. Clay puppet Mr Bill is sent to a psychiatrist when he is discovered drinking rye in an allyway with grafitti saying No Bills. Dr. I. M. Häns puts him under hypnosis & asks if he had any bad childhood memories. Mr Bill remembers his father was decapitated in Sluggoville. Häns asks if he had trouble during the holidays or a bad Christmas. Mr Bill recalls Sluggo dressed as Santa bringing a train that crushed him. Mr Bill is asked if he has any nightmares. Mr Bill sees himself flushed down a toilet & a circle of hands saying Sieg Heil. Mr Bill is taken out of hypnosis, told he has hand paranoia & is given a lobotomy by associate Dr. Sluggo. – Walter Williams, Mr Bill Gets Help, Saturday Night Live, NBC: National Broadcasting Company: USA: 197

Camp to exterminate Polish children who could not be Germanized. The ghetto had an Arbeitsressorte: industrial complex inside creating a $14,000,000 profit. 12-hour days, producing garments, wood, metalwork, electronics for the German military. Children forced into extermination trucks. Others were thrown from windows to their death.

Human experiments, organ harvesting at Kochanowka Hospitol. 1944: Himmler orders the Einsatzgrüppen: Death Commandos. 900 people hide in the ruins. City declared Judenrein: Free of Jews. This resulted in the death of 553,000 people.

KL Warshau / Pawiak-Warsaw Koncenträk 24 Kreuz, punch-card technology used by the Nazis to organize the Polish railways & make the trains run on time to Auschwitz & Treblinka as well as categorization. Print shop for the punch cards at 6 Rymarska Street across the street from the Warsaw Ghetto. The welfare office punchcards were sent to the new expanded sorting office in Lichterfeld Warsaw: Built by the Tsar in 1829. Used as a transfer camp to Siberia. After Poland regained independence in 1918 it became the main prison for male criminals. Female prison was G´siówka. After the German invasion of Poland in 1939 it was turned into a German GeStaPo prison & then part of the KL Warshau: Warsaw Ghetto. 37,000+ shot to death, disease, forced labor, starvation, 60,000+ death marched to other camps. April 1943: A revolt took place in the ghetto under Mordecai Anielecz when SS Death Heads General Juergen Stroop (tried &

216

hanged in Warsaw in 1951) attempted to raze the ghetto & deport them Treblinka. The train consisted of 60 closed freight cars fully loaded with people including babies. By the time the cars got to Treblinka many had died of chlorine gas. July 30, 1944 Wilhelm Koppe Goecke orders the camp liquidated 2000 men & 400 women sent to Ravensbrück, remaining prisoners shot & the buildings blown up.

Bialystok [June 28, 1941: Red Friday: NAZI's burn the city. 1000+ Jews forced into the synagogue & killed. Orders issued that any Jewish person in Poland found outside a ghetto will be shot. In August 1943 Jews rebel against the NAZI's in the Bialystok Ghetto & shot to death] 1266: Papal nuncio Guido authorized theft of Jewish real-estate, one synagogue per town, mandatory red badge, banned from public view during Christian holidays & excommunication for those inviting Jewish people to parties

1407: Riot of Kraków Priest Budek has Jews killed, property destroyed & their children baptized

Bochnia Ghetto [Kraków. In 1942 12 year old Leo Fischelberg watched children rounded up by NAZI's & loaded into open trucks from his hiding place. NAZI's shot the grieving mothers with machine guns]

The Great Escape: March 24, 1944, 76 allied prisoners escaped through a 110-m long tunnel. 73 were recaptured within two weeks. 50 of them were executed by order of Hitler] Polenlager [Polish People Camps]

In 440 of these camps, at least 1.5 million Poles were set to hard labor. Many of these camps were transient in nature, being opened, & closed according to the labour needs of the occupiers. – Wikipedia.

VL Vernichtungslanger: Extermination Camp

AEG Todt: Teutonic Order Death Camps

1939: Blitzkrieg: Lightening War: Invasion of Poland. All Jewish banking accounts frozen, schools closed deportations, house arrests, street raids, & Jewish Councils set up. 1941: yellow identity cards issued. Death penalty was applied to all that shelter the Jews or keep their belongings.

The Final Solution: Verdict of LG Hagen AZ: II Ks 1/64: Dr. Buhler's request for extermination of all Jews by the end of 1942. Warehouses of the body-snachers where hundreds of prisoners worked frantically to sort, segregate & classify the clothes & the food & the valuables of those whose bodies were still burning, whose ashes would soon be used as a fertilizer. Nearby was another mountain, of blankets this time, fifty thousand of them, maybe one hundred thousand. Dr. Horst Schumann sterilizes hundreds of men, women, & children with radiation X-ray burns. Gasses them. Cuts off testicles for examination SS Hauptsturmführer: Dr Josef Mengele &

Irma Griese the Angel of Death: the Blond Beast & the Queen of Auschwitz torture, vivisection. Auschwitz II-Birkenau / Brzezinka [Gas chambers. bodies thrown to the dogs. Aktion Höß: Preparation of Hungarians for the gas chambers. In his autobiography Höß says 2.5 million were killed according to Eichmann. Annaliese Frank's stepsister Eva Schloß survived. Eva's autobiography of 1988 says an Oberführerin called her a protected Jew because her cousin worked as a nurse under Mengele. Anne Frank's mom died there. Eva's mother survived & married Otto Frank], Auschwitz III-Buna-Monowitz / Buna-Monowice [IG Farben chemical gas manufacture. Buna synthetic-rubber works. 940 deaths: 1.5 million Jews, 76, 000 French, 150 000 Polish, 23 000 Czech, 15 000 Russians. Hollerith Büro at German Civil Workers Camp 7, Barracks 18 under Herr Hirsch, Herr Husch, & card index systems runner Eduard Müller. Müller is described as a rabid NAZI who enjoyed harming inmates, fat, aging, ill kempt man, with brown hair & brown eyes who stank like a polecat. Lublin, was famous in 1530, for the Jewish printing houses. Second largest Nazi Death Camp in Europe after Auschwitz. 25,000 killed per day. 400,000+. 7 gas chambers were using Zyklon B & Carbon Monoxide, 2 wooden gallows, crematorium with 5 furnaces. SS-Brigadeführer Odilo Globocnik under Himmler with SS-Sturmbannführer Hermann Höfle, responsible for Reinhold Felix: collection of the victims' valuables. Clothes, gold, money, jewelry, & belongings stored, sorted at the unused hangars of Lublin Airfield, put into the Reichsbank. Train brought into camp by specially selected team of railroad workers, gassing, gold teeth extracted,]

Belzec II: [Extermination Center: 15,000 killed per day under Aktion T-4 Euthanasia Program. (T-4 stands for the office's address Tiergartenstraße 4 in Berlin). 100 Totenjuden: Jews of Death forced to drag the corpses from the gas chambers & to carry them to the open ditches covering up them up with sand, while thick black blood floods the ground like a lake, killed each day & replaced by new arrivals. SS-Scharfuehrer Heinrich Gley testified to incinerating corpses day & night without interruption with an average of 500,000 corpses within five months between November 1942-March 1943. Incinerators were capable of burning, 2000 corpses within 24 hours. VL: 350,000 died with carbon monoxide in gas vans. Corpses incinerated with gasoline. Remaining bones placed on thin metal sheets, crushed & shaked through a narrow-mesh metal sieve. Ashes mixed with sand & garbage. Corpses at Kulmhof, were burnt with bombs; then on wood fires straight from the gas chambers & existing mass graves

VL Treblinka- the Perfect Extermination Camp
Not far from Malkinia on the main Warsaw-Bialystok lines near the Malkinia-Siedlce line. Director Kurt Franz sentenced to life in 1965. 25,000 killed per day. 1, 400,000 minimum est (witnesses were killed), starvation, urine drinking, poison gas. Gas chambers in a massive brick building in the center. Access paths,

including the tube, in Treblinka named Street to Heaven by the SS-men. Treblinka I [Infirmary, receiving area, Sonderkommandos unload train, undress passengers, thrown them in ditches, shoot & burn bodies. Others rushed into the gas chambers with attack dogs, whips & iron bars. 10,000-12,000 per day], Treblinka II [500 prisoners, gas chambers that can kill 3000 in two hours & furnaces, dentists pull out gold teeth of the dead with pliers. Totenjuden: Jews of Death, who clean the gas chambers, sift & bury the ashes. 1500 men work crews replaced every three to five days. SS Oberscharfuehrer Heinrich Matthes & Floß oversee corpse burning]

In Portugal [Lusitania: Black Raven, Bone Chapels]

1932: António Salazar's New State International Police for the Defense of the State, Chapel of Bones Church of Sao Francisco, Évora [Home of the Tribunal of the Inquisition. Hundreds tried & burnt at the stake. 1460: bones of more than 5,000 people on interior walls, ceilings, and archways. Cobwebbed skulls stacked to reach the ceiling], Faro Carmelite church [built entirely of bones. 1,250 skeletons. The floor is made up of gravestones covering even more bodies.]

In Puerto Rico: [Borike'n]. 1493: Columbus names the island San Juan Bautista: St. John the Baptist. 1555: Sir Francis Drake, a slave trader in the Carribean, invades with the Count of Cumberland

Spanish-American War: Treaty of Paris: USA receive Puerto Rico as war payment from Spain.

In Qatar Colonial, 1916: British Protectorate. 1971: Independance

1990: Gulf War Qatari air force base [1990: Used to attack Iraqi forces. Qatar took part in the bombing of Iraqi military targets & in the ground offensive to liberate Kuwait in early 1991.]

République Centrafricaine Mass Graves.

1910-1959: Part of French Equitorial Africa: David Dacko. In 1966, His human rights violations (which are said to have included cannibalism & the feeding of school children to crocodiles, amongst others)

[In Zaïre]. Belgian Congo Camps deConcentration

Belgian King Leopold II assasinates King M'Siri & rapes the area's mineral wealth. He hires the British Army to murder millions of Africans in the Belgian Congo in his quest for rubber. He seizes Chad. England seizes Nigeria. Germany seizes Tangayika & Zanzibar. Italy seizes Somalia & Ethiopia.

He charged that Belgians were aiding rebel Katangans [province seceeded]. Tipp the slaver from Zanzibar(0 of the Spice Islands, as governor. Cannibalism, beheading, hands cut off & used as currency]

Eastern Congo [1998: Uprising against government. Rebels backed by troops from Rwanda & Uganda vs Kabila's Angola, Chad, Namibia, Zimbabwe forces. 1999: Chad removes troops. 2000: UN Peacekeeping Force.

219

Goma Camp [1995: First Congo War: Watutsi People leave Zaire on penalty of death. 4.4 million+ dead. Dissappearances tortures, killing. 1997: President Mobutu Sese Seko flees & is replaced by Laurent Kabila, a rebel assassinated by his own bodyguards. 1998: Second Congo War. 5,500 UN PeaceKeeping Forces. 2004 estimated 1000 dead per day with 3 million+ killed for gold & diamonds. Civilians fleeing to forest: dying of malaria, measles, and diarrhea.]

Slavery in [French Congo]

Lake formed by the widening of the Congo River. Triangular slave trade, Point-Noir; Oyo; Bateke M'Bochi, and the Sangha People

République du Madagascar: End of the Earth Vichy Camp de Concentration.

SE African country made up Madagascar Island & tiny surrounding islands: Moro Islands Malagasy language resembles Malay & Indonesian

1896-1960: French Colony.WWII internment camps. Textile wages are 37 cents an hour: contracts from Victoria are Secret and The Gap

République du Togo Mass Graves

Porajmos [The Devouring]: Romani term for the Holocaust

Lier acted with the full knowledge of IBM president. And then they came for the Gypsies: The Legacy of Death's Calculator © 2004

1941 'Romania's massive census was so sophisticated it even enumerated which Roma Gypsies were already refugees temporarily absent or already interned in a concentration camp. Those afraid to admit their extraction settled gypsies Counting officials & inspectors received orders to make the official entries according to the countees' wishes, but add a comment stating that in their opinion or in the general opinion of the community they were considered to be Gypsies. Hence, the IBM tabulations would record them as Gypsy regardless of the ethnic box checked. He concluded, The total number of Gypsies (without counting Gypsy half-breeds) is estimated to be 300,000. 25,000+ Gypsies rounded up pursuant to the Romanian Interior Minister's order #70S/1942. Roadblocks set up on the outskirts of town as gendarmes, with lists of names, fanned out to arrest the Gypsies, deport them in trains, scheduled & tracked by Hollerith machines.

Curatirea Terenului [Cleansing of the Ground]

Ion Antonescu: ordered on-the-spot extermination of Jews. Deputy Prime Minister killed between 150,000 & 160,000 Jews during July & August 1941. Ion Antonescu's goal was to have all the Jews of Romania annihilated in less than a year Bukovina [Soviets invade: Zionists & Enemies of the State deported to Siberia. Romanian NAZIs Infantry Battalion 16, Maj. Valeriu Carp, kills the Red Army & thousands of Jews in the villages. Property stolen], Chernovtsy [ghetto. Einsatzgruppe D], Cotmani, Kishinev, Lujeni, Marculesti, Rezina [liquidated], Soroca [80 percent of Jewish residents murdered],

Storojineti, Transnistria [Death march of 1,600 per day], Vertujeni [daily death toll 170, starvation, torture, rape. Antonescu's forces massacre peaceful crowds. 360+ men, women, & children hunted down by armed gangs. No Legionaries killed. 1989: Thousands of demonstrators killed. Cosauti Forest, Dniester [Roads filled with the corpses of Jews who had been shot], Timisoara [1989: Hundreds killed in demostrations for an improved standard of living.]

In Russia [People Murder]

Borisovo [Mass grave October 1944], Grozny [refugee camps. Government headquarters bombed [1940: NKVD head Beria massacres 25,700+ under Stalin], Kharkov [Hausser. SS throw grenades at a military field hospital and the people inside are burnt alive (130)], Saratov [toxic gas invented here. German chemical weapons research & manufacture]

Vernichtungslager [Extermination Camp].

Katorga [Concentration Camps]

'Molotov claimed in radio broadcasts that the Soviet Union was not dropping bombs, but rather delivering food to the starving Finns, the Finns responded by saluting the advancing tanks with Molotov cocktails [a.k.a Napalm: naptholine-aluminum soap powder + palm oil + gasoline] ' – Wikipedia

1921-1938 League of Nations' High Commission for Refugees: assist people who fled the Russian Revolution of 1917 & the subsequent civil war. In 1923, the mandate of the Commission was expanded to include Armenians.

1945: Yalta Conference: Millions of former Russian citizens forcefully repatriated (against their will) into the USSR. Ostarbeiters: Eastern Workslaves, Soviet POWs, & Vlasov men put under the jurisdiction of SMERSH (Death to Spies). – Wikipedia 1889: Kara Tragedy Woman prisoner flogged to death. 18 prisoners take poison & 6 of them die], 1703: Named Petrograd: Saint Petersburg, then Ivangorod, then Leningrad, then Stalingrad. WWII: population transfers: 63,000+ fled to Finland during World War II, sent back to Stalin & executed as unreliables. Secret police take people away to a remote location to be killed in the night. Kolyma [forced labor in gold & diamond mines. Called the White Crematorium: the land of White Death. Stalin had wooden watchtowers pulled down, police women disguised as swineherds & prisoners hidden when US Vice-President Henry Wallace visited in 1944], Berelakh, Magadan [Trans-Siberian Railway with a station at Vladivostok carries slave labor in goldmines discovered in 1925. Polish, German, Romanian, Lithuanian, Latvian, Mongolian, Chinese, Korean, Afghan, Armenian & Japanese POWS. Dismantled late 60s. Government records banished survivor's victims of severe frostbite. Dead remained forever in mass graves, dug into the permafrost, or had their bodies buried under rocks or carried away by spring flood to the Arctic Sea], Sevvoslag: NE Camp [mass executions of the inmates ordered by S. N. Garanin, Chief NKVD Officer], Vladivostok [1860: Korean border. Trans-Siberian Railroad], Maxim Gorky [gold mine], Laso, Chukhots, Maldyak, Komsomolets, Yoshkar-Ola, Sukhobezvodnaya [corrective labor-camp. Sector 4: transit camp. Barbed wire and dogs, in-between], Vorkuta [1932: Stalin sent his daughter Svetlana's fiancé Alexei Kapler there]. Wrangel Island [Ferdinand von Wrangel]

Sharashka GULAG

General Valentin Kravchenko

Scientists & engineers prisoners picked from other camps & given relatively better conditions in exchange for their slave-like work on scientific & technological problems for the state – Wikipedia

Rwanda [Deutsch-Ostafrika: German East Africa /

WWI: Seized by Belgium. People taxed, forced into slave corvée labor on coffee plantations. 'Genocide is justified in the fight against the enemy. Militia kills 800,000+ Tutsis & Hutu moderates in the Rwandan Genocide: French send in peacekeeping troops in Opération Turquoise. 2 million+ Hutus flee.], Butare & Gitarama [Kambanda distributes small arms ammunition. He confessed that the government organized the genocide in advance. His lawyer argued that he was a puppet of the military, which dragged him from his bank, after killing the previous Prime Minister], Lake Kivu [dead bodies thrown into the lake. 1994: 1/2 million people massacred in less than four months]

In Saudi Arabia War,

1960: OPEC. 1990: Persian Gulf War Khafji [1991: Invaded by Iraqi troops. 1991: Iraq launches Scud missiles at populated areas in Israel & Saudi Arabia, terrorizing the populations of targeted cities & killing a number of people in both Israel & Saudi Arabia. – World Book Encyclopedia © 1998], Mecca [The Holy City. The Five Pillars of Islam: The Hajj, or pilgrimage to Mecca. When completed al-Hajj added to name. The sacred Black Stone sent from Allah to the Prophet Abraham by the Angel Gabriel, is the stone to which one turns five times each day to pray.], Yethrib-Medina [North of Mecca. Hegira the trip from Mecca to Medina]

Sleabaght [Slavery]

Mossbank Industrial School [Hogganfield. 600+ destitute children forced into domestic slavery], Easter Ross [1849-1946: Arthurville. Children starved to death on potatoes, pea soup, treacle-water, and oatmeal. Area now owned by Mohamed al-Fayed of Harrod's]

Eaddeeyn-Vaaish [Mass Graves]

Edinburgh Theatre [Mass Grave], Inverness-Culloden Moor [Fleet Street was overlooked by the skulls of the Scots rebels decapitated after 1745, skulls kept there till 1772], Inverness [mass starvation. whole families died of cholera in   their beds]

Thie NY Moght [Place of Death]

Hitler told newspapers in Germany that Unity was a perfect specimen of Aryan womanhood. She was given the gold Nazi party badge, the highest honour Hitler could bestow. Her sister Diana married British fascist leader Sir Oswald Mosley. Unity died in 1948 of complications of a self-inflicted bullet to the brain. Black Isle [1859-1946: Ness Road. Children starved to death In the Laundry. Mass graves known as Agricultural Improvements], Co. Sutherland [Sutherland Mormaerdom]: Sutherland-Stonehaven Workhouse [1863: Laundry, childrens' wards. Now Migdale Hospital], In Glasgow: Co Lanark [Lannraig]: Cambusnethan [Inmates stripped naked, starved to death on broth, whipped, & drowned in cold baths], Dalziel [1903: Laundry, disinfector], Monklands [Two workhouses. Child murder], Town's Hospital Inc. [1730], Glasgow City Poorhouse [1809: 1500 beds], and Glasgow Barony–Barnhill [1853: Mass graves. site of railway station. Children starved to death on thC-Plan of oatmeal, bread, & milk. Ayr [1756: 150+ inmates. H-Block childrens' quarters. Inmates dying from: pneumonia, pleurisy, phthisis, cancer, paralysis from starvation, senile decay: wet cases], Cunninghame [1857-1996: Irvine. Punishment beatings], Maybole [1867-1918], Co. Renfrew [Siorrachd Rinn Friù]: Paisley Asylum-Abbey Parish-Renfrewshire Abbey [1849: 650+ inmates. Oakum picking, Infirmary], Busby [1906], Greenock Parochial Lunatic Asylum [1868-1941: Starved to death on broth, bread, & herring, fed twice a week. Coal shoveling. Girls covered with lice eggs, insects, & vermin. 1934: Inmates drugged with thormaldithyde & bromide by nuns. Half of the male inmates from North Uist], Outer Hebrides [na h-Eileanan Siar: Western Isles]Glas na Goirteann: The Minch: Lews Workhouse [1894: Isle of Lewis & Harris: Lewis na Hearish. Operational through 1942], Isle of Taransay: Thunder Island [human bones protrude from sand on Peible Beach], Scalpay, Barra Isles: Barra [The MacNeil landlords since the 12th century cleared the people from the black houses named after the coal smoke for sheep farming. The farmers and fisherman were sent to Canada, Ireland, and the United States]. Kisimul: Castle Island [Owned by John Allen MacNeil who inherited the castle from his father Robert Lister MacNeil in 1937]. Vatersay [Rusted landmine shells from WWII, Memorial commemorates the 450 people who died aboard the Highland Clearances emigrant ship. Long Island Workhouse: [1851: Highlanders seized and led to the ships in chains. Placed in the steerage & died of disease], Hirta Island [Now occupied by the military & scientists for the Hebrides missile tracking range who do test firings], Between 1830 -1843, 80% of infants dying of tetanus. The last 36 remaining inhabitants were evacuated to the Scottish mainland.

In Galloway: Dumfries Hospital [Kirkpatrick-Fleming 1861. Co. Fife [Fife Mormaerdon] In Kirkudbrightshire (pronounced Kir-COO-bri-shir) Kirkcudbright Workhouse [1849-1950], Rinns of Galloway [1850: Stranraer, Wigtownshire. 381+ inmates. Described in 1946 as worn-out, dreary without proper sanitation, or heating]. Inmates starved to death on gruel. Slavery in the laundries & garden], Kircaldy 1895 Aberdeen-Buchan Workhouse 1867-1946: Inmates starved, forced to grow potatoes, turnips, and oats. Cesspool. Mass graves. Pathways made from cinders of the workhouse boilers.

Sénégal [Senegambia / French West Africa]

Fagaala [People Murder]

1492: Portuguese Colonial slavery

1960: Independance

Seychelles: Jean Moreau de Séchelles. Slavery

In the Indian Ocean just north of Madagascar. Sierra Leone: In Portuguese Slavery

1524-5s: Brazilian slave trade

1808: English diamond mines. Jamaican maroons transported into the country

1832: St. Kitts Rebellion, La Amistad Revolt: Cinque/Singbe, an African headman from Sierra Leone kidnapped, kills the captain & crew. Cinque & 38 of his followers arrested with piracy at Long Island their owners sue for their return. According to Anti-Slavery International the average slave in 1850 fetches $40,000

Bunce Island [18th century British slave castle that sent many of its captives to Georgia & South Carolina where American rice planters paid a premium for experienced slaves from Africa's Rice Coast].

Freetown [City for former slaves living in London. 1989: Foday Sankoh's wars against the government with child soldiers. 500 UN Peacekeepers held hostage. 2 million people, 1/3+ of the population, displaced refugees in neighboring countries, 200,000+ dead, others disfigured & amputated with machetes. 2001: Sankoh indicted by UN-War Crimes Commission.]

Blood Diamonds: Child-slaves work under armed guard for two cups of rice a day.

Slovakia: Slovenska Republica [Czechoslovakia]

Koncentrák [Concentration Camp]

Mnozieni Umor [Mass Graves]

Yugoslav Watson AG

13th SS Division 'Handschar' SS: Dieter Wisliceny

1918: NAZI Hussar general Joseph "Tito" Broz declares himself president, Slovenia part of the Kingdom of the Serbs, Croats, & Slovenes, later renamed Yugoslavia. 1946: Slovenia a republic in the Yugoslav state. 1980: Tito dies.

1991: Independance

1667-1975: Dutch take control & give the English the colony of New Amsterdam / New York.The official language is Dutch. 1980, a group of Suriname's armed forces seize control of the country & abolish the Parliament.

South Africa [Cape Colony / Rhodesia: Cecil   Rhodes / Zululand]

Mfecane [Great Crushing Death March]

1488: Portuguese Bartolomeu Dias seizes Capetown

1647: Dutch East India Company 's Jan van Riebeeck exterminates the Khoikhoi: Men of Men

1715: Smallpox war commandos exterminate Bushmen/San & import slaves from India, Indonesia, Madagascar, & Mozambique to work on plantations

1877-1881: First Boer War: (pron. bawr) 19th century Netherlands war with England over land

1899-1902: Second Boer War: Concentration camp first used in 1900 to describe open-air camps in South Africa where the English kept Boer prisoners of war. 1948-1991: Apartheid: Seperateness in Afrikaans-Dutch: black, white, mixed race, Asian.

1994-1999: President Nelson Rolihlahla Mandela (imprisoned 1962-1990) Aliwal North Camp Balmoral Camp [110,000 Dutch & 107,000 Africans, starvation, farm destruction, disease, fed meat & flour crawling with maggots, poisoned with copper sulfate, ground glass, fishhooks & razor blades. Transportation in open cattle trucks]

Barberton, Belfast, Bethulie, and Bloemfontain: Fountain of Flowers Camp [13 toilets for 3,500 people, no water or soap they are luxury items. The judicial capital of South Africa]

Brandfort [Apartheid instituted. Nelson Mandela is Thembu Royalty, a subgroup of the Xhosa]

Johannesburg [Gauteng Province. Whipped until dead. Survivors forced to work in mines & shot dead if protest].

Potchefstroom Camp [Lloyd George says 450,000 women & children killed per year. Estimated 3 million Boer dead]

Salisbury [Capital of South Africa. Riots in 1965. Unemployment has risen from 17 percent in 1995 to about 30 percent.]

1948: Korea liberated from Japan, but split in half. USA took the South & Russia the North. Then North Korea invaded South Korea & UN Forces captured Seoul in 1951. Start of the Cold War.

Spain, [Concentration Camps]

The poison they use is made from the seeds of the yew tree, a plant with mythic significance.

929 AD-1031 AD: Moroccan Umayyad Caliphate: Moroccan general Tariq ibi z-Zaid names it Al-Andaluz. Jabalu t-tariq, Gibraltar named after him.

1478-1492: Spanish Inquistion: King Ferdinand VI of Aragon & Queen Isabella I of Castile persecute & expel Jews & Muslims from Spain

Guernica [Basque country. 51 biplanes bomb it. Casualties estimated at 1,000,000+]. I saw the Basque protestors at Googenheim Museum, for release of their freedom fighters.

In Sri Lanka: Blessed Isle [Ceylon]. Imperialism

1537: Vasco de Gama voyages to Sri Lanka. Diego Fernandez Correa writes in the Luciads, that he cut off the hands, ears, & noses of 800 Indian Muslims, tied up the rest of them, & set their ships on fire

1948: Independence from England. English replaced with Sinhala & Tamil. Kandy means the Kings of Ceylon, & their flag is a lion on a red background. Kandy Temple has a tooth of the Buddha. Anuradhapura [Royal City. Pilgrims view a sapling of the sacred bo tree where Buddha obtained enlightenment], I implemented the program for major Electrification of the Budha Gaya town and the actual Bodhee tree, during 1950 international Budha Festival there.
 Colombo [Portuguese invaded in 1517. Named the capital city Colombo after Christopher Columbus. Precious jewels: rubies, sapphires, pearls, spices], Jaffna [Professor Brett Wallach: Tamil Tigers fighting for autonomy since 1983. 60,000+ dead. 2002: Ceasefire & peace talks] Sudan: Black in Arabic [Mass Graves]. 350 AD: Kush Kingdom ends under Alexander the Great.

White Nile & Blue Nile branches meet here. Downtown streets are laid out with union jacks. Machine guns placed in the center of each cross], Torit [Civil War: 1955-present. 500,000+ killed before temporary cease-fire in 1972.]

Displacement Camps

2002 drought has 1/4 of the population needing emergency food. 34% unemployment rate. Sugar plantations, wood pulp, and mining. 40% of adults infected with HIV, making it the world's highest AIDS rate.

In Sweden [Mass Grave]

1520: Blood Bath: Massacre of Swedish nobles after the coronation of Christian II King of Denmark, Sweden [Scania] & Norway.

Russian army invades Sweden, conducts biological germ warfare by flinging plague-infected corpses over the city walls]

Folkmord= [People Murder].

1939: IBM Sweden sells 1.9 million punch cards to Demark, 1.3 million to Finland, 696,000 to Norway, 1 million to Yugoslavia, 700,000 to Spain & 251,000 to Hungary, enablic data to catch Jews

Doverstorp [Internment camp]

Die Grabeln (Mass Graves)

Julius Caesar attacks the Helvetti under Orgetorix who are migrating to France. Caesar's 8 legions kill 60% of the 470,000 population & the rest escape into Helvetia, the mountains of Switzerland

Dominican Churchyard, Basel [Plague], Dominican Churchyard, Berne [Plague], Le Bridge du Moulin, Lucerne [Plague], Jesuits College,   Lucerne [Plague], Segendorf [1710 Plague]

Concentration Camps: Swiss Aid Society for Jewish Refugees

KriPo: KriminalPolizei: Criminal Police: Arthur Nebe: head of the Criminal State Police of all Germany, Austria, Switzerland & the Berliner Sturmabteilung: Storm Troopers. Red Cresent Concentration Camps

Occupied by France after WWI as French Mandate of Syria. Armenian Genocide: The mountain of Ashur is the border between Assyria & Armenia.

At the segregated Oriental School established in 1884], 6 Colored Schools [1864: San Francisco, Sacramento, Marysville, San Jose, Stockton, & Petaluma. Black teachers barred as public school teachers except in El Centro], Sacramento [Indian, Chinese, Japanese, Mongolian, Filipino children barred from public school through 1947], Sherman Indian High School [Riverside California's urban Indians are unknown, uncountable, an enigma, said Indian Health Service statistician Lorraine McCall. 'Everybody knows there's this mystery urban Indian population, but when they go to Congress for funding, they have little hard data.

In Montana: Spanish for Mountain Fergus Co. Poorhouse [closed 1965], Yellowstone-Riverside-Billings, Silver Bow Co. Poorfarm Inc. [1879. Trolleys called Cemetery Cars transported thousands of the dead through Montana Street to the Cemetery. The North Coast line of the Northern Pacific Railroad stopped there four times a day. Pestilence House. Babies died of Smallpox. Now NCAT: National center for Appropriate Technology], Forestvale Montana [Lewis & Co. Chinese burial ground]

Salem [1887-1985. largest off reservation boarding school. 903 students from 90 different tribes. punishment beatings. 189 gravestones. other bodies sent home for burial.

Forbidden City. Shanghai Tunnels [1850-1941: No Negro, Chinaman, or mulatto shall have the right of suffrage. People falling through deadfalls: trapdoors into underground tunnels from above ground & being sold as ship galley slaves. While they were waiting for a ship to come to port, the prisoners were kept in brick cells with no lights and very narrow bars. During Prohibition, saloons occupied a portion of the Underground. Crimps or white slavers sold thousands of women into prostitution. They were picked up at dances, forcibly grabbed off the streets, or slipped knockout drops in saloon, pool hall, & gambling parlor drinks. Babies born to prostitutes sold by James Turk, The Father of Portland Crimping. – Shanghai Tunnel FAQ], Sucker: Lake Oswego [Boarding houses, brothels, and opium dens grab men for slavery. Bartenders paid by the ship captains. In 1897, four men deserted The Arago & found guilty by the US Supreme Court, even though they claimed they had been sold into involuntary servitude. When the Chinese Exclusion Act was lifted in 1965 many Gurus came west. They appealed to people appalled by the French-Indo China / Vietnam War & created a surge for things Eastern.] 1853: Illinois Black Code: Black immigrants & travellers who remain in Illinois for more than 10 days are fined $100 or

227

more. Those who are unable to pay are sold into indentured servitude at public auction. With this act Illinois was able to practice a form of slavery upon free blacks that entered the state without having to officially declare itself a slave state. Illinois lawmakers were able to get around the Northwest Ordinance's prohibition against slavery, which exempted forced servitude as punishment for a criminal offense.

Minnesota: Occoquan [jail. site of women's suffrage protest in 1918] Nebraska: 1854: Rosebud [housing monies stolen, children kidnapped, people starved, denied medical treatment, internment without trial]. Kansas: -Nebraska Act 1854 [Opened the area to settlement & allowed slavery to be decided by popular sovereignty. Lawless mayhem known as "Bleeding Kansas" took place. 1864: Tribes massacred under territorial military commander Colonel John Chivington & villages razed. Indian Territory: Oklahoma: Red People: 1541 [Mexican Empire] Tempted by stories of a city of gold called Quivira, Francisco Vasquez de Coronado led an expedition eastward across the Pecos River. He wandered through present-day Texas, Oklahoma & Kansas, Nance Indian Boarding School [1912: Malaria]. FDR. The great Deprssion, 35% unemployment,

The great WWI, The Prohibition, Mile Long Poverty, and Food/Coupon lines, the hatred against the filthy rich, were not the only challenges faces by the 4 term presidency. There was, the Kansas Crime Wave, 4 years after the crash of the stock market. The Government Police force and the newly formed FBI under the inexperienced, J.Edgar Hoover (who never carried a gun) was under siege, and virtually paralysed. They were no matches to the notorious, John Dillinger, BOONNEY&CLYDE, Baby-face George Nelson, the Machine-gun Kelley, to name a few. They learnt and earned Ph.D in the art and science of advanced Bank Robberies and robbed the National Guards stockpile of advanced modern weapons. With tons of cash they bought the fastest get away trucks. They were cheared by the crowds for what was considered to be Robin Hood activity of daring daylight "Robbing the Rich," The rich and not them were the real criminals.

Essex Prison [Small Pox Hospital, Lunatic Asylum] Colored Home [for sick, aged & poor blacks], Ossining [Sing Sing Penitentary], NY Counties Cemeteries: Albany, Bloomingdale, Chautauqua, Rockingham [unmarked graves] Trust imports Chinese slaves for the rice fields. 1874: Klu Klux Klan 1913: Rice moves to Texas & Arkansas.

Kuuraya [Mass Murder] 1995: 5 million+ people are starving. Amnesty International report torture.

I see these things with an intense joy,

And while I observe, there is no observer,

almost a beauty almost like love.

For an instant I am absent, myself and my problems, my

anxieties, my troubles: nothing but this wonder exists.

Krishnamurti

AUTHOR: **GO PAL**

Was brought up by his Canny Nanny with lots of fresh air and love.

From a tough childhood under kinder and lonely skies, he boomed into a ripened world class citizen. Blessed with an evergreen memory housed in an over tasked brain, he stored millions of real incidences and fascinating stories which were transferred to four. books simultaneously. Each were well planned but GADDAFI UP-Close was well timed and hit the bookstores even before Gaddafi was caught, assassinated and sodomized- (what a shame!)

This present book "LIBYA'S DESTINY POST GADDAFI"highlights my four years working as a top executive of EXXON when he personally met GADDAFI. It also illuminates the future of Libya after Gaddafi under a variety of circumstances E.g. The changing politics in Europe and USA, as well as the effects of the so called revolution.

VA YA CON DIOS is about my child-cum-adulthood(Spanish title by an Indian author, and written in English).

My book "POLITICS OF CONVENIENCE UPSET THE BALANCE OF POWER" is very current and includes chapters like HEGEMONY, PENDULUM THEORY, THE BRAIN(DAMAG), OBAMA AND THE FIRST FIRST LADY, and much more. Remember an eye for an eye makes the whole world go blind.

www.authorgopalbooks.com

Please visit above web site for details